D.K.'s Sushi Chronicles
from Hawai'i

D.K.'s Sushi Chronicles from Hawai'i

RECIPES FROM SANSEI SEAFOOD
RESTAURANT & SUSHI BAR

DAVE "D.K." KODAMA with Bonnie Friedman

Photography by JOHN DE MELLO

TEN SPEED PRESS
Berkeley | Toronto

Ten Speed Press
Box 7123
Berkeley, California 94707
www.tenspeed.com

Distributed in Australia by Simon & Schuster Australia, in Canada by Ten Speed Press Canada, in New Zealand by Southern Publishers Group, in South Africa by Real Books, and in the United Kingdom and Europe by Airlift Book Company.

Jacket and text design by Toni Tajima
Photography by John De Mello
Food & prop styling by Nina Pfaffenbach
Photography assistance by Brad Goda
Photos on pages 3 and 7 courtesy of the author
Photos on pages 60, 147, 205 by Toni Tajima

Some of the recipes in this book include raw eggs, meat, or fish. When these foods are consumed raw, there is always the risk that bacteria, which is killed by proper cooking, may be present. For this reason, when serving these foods raw, always buy certified salmonella-free eggs and the freshest meat and fish available from a reliable grocer, storing them in the refrigerator until they are served. Because of the health risks associated with the consumption of bacteria that can be present in raw eggs, meat, and fish, these foods should not be consumed by infants, small children, pregnant women, the elderly, or any people who may be immunocompromised.

The author would like to thank Dean and Ray Okimoto at Nalo Farms, Local Island Fresh Edibles; Jo Rasmussen and Glenn Tanoue at Tropic Fish; and Frankie Sekiya at Frankie's Nursery for supplying some of the ingredients photographed in this book.

Library of Congress Cataloging-in-Publication Data on file with the publisher

ISBN 1-58008-467-2

Printed in China
First printing, 2003

1 2 3 4 5 6 7 8 9 10 — 08 07 06 05 04 03

For my family
Issei, Nisei, Sansei, Yonsei
Generations past, present, future

Contents

Acknowledgments

SUCCESSFUL BUSINESSES, especially restaurants, are always the result of what in Hawai'i is known as *lau lima*, "many hands"—and, in our case, heads and hearts.

As I was getting started in this business, a lot of wonderful people shared their knowledge and experience with me, and my sincere thanks go to them. Robert Peterson, Peter Chalman, and Jim Phelan taught me what it takes to manage a restaurant, then Jack Ichikawa trusted me with the management of his restaurant in Aspen. Julie Murad-Weiss and Peter O'Grady opened my eyes to the world of gourmet cuisine. Casey Koffman let me play at her sushi bar, and Kenichi Kanada taught me how to play at the sushi bar. Master Sushi Chef Katsuhiko Sato taught me the fine points of Japanese cooking. Bev and Joe Gannon gave me an opportunity to hone my sushi skills, while Nobu Matsuhisa, the "guru," provided all the inspiration.

Alice and Dwayne Bower helped me to find my first Sansei Seafood Restaurant & Sushi Bar location. Don Young, Bob McNatt, Gary Planos, Bob Derks, Russ Johnson, Wayne Hidani, and David Sozner of Kapalua Land Company believed in us wholeheartedly as they handed over the keys to our new restaurant. Gary Gifford and everyone at Maui Land & Pineapple were also behind us. Kevin Baptiste and Edwin Tokuoka of Bank of Hawai'i believed in us enough to lend us the money . . . but not without a cosigner! That was my good friend, Patricia Steele. Bank of Hawai'i's Dancine Takahashi showed us a lot of aloha, helped us through the whole loan process, and guided us through our first years. She still does. Willis Choy and Penny Uncles worked long and hard on our business plan, and did it all for love. We're proud and lucky to call these great folks our good friends.

I will be forever grateful to the loyal customers who have frequented our Kapalua restaurant from the very beginning. I am your humble servant, always.

Andy Friedlander is a man who makes things happen at Colliers Monroe Friedlander. Buzz Wo, Corinne Arquero, Jenai and Roger Wall, and the entire Sullivan family helped make Kihei a reality. Mitch Kysar, our contractor, and our architects, Gerald Gambill and Robert Domingo, did a wonderful job on the design and construction.

There are many other people who have helped along the way. Larry Fujino, our CPA, and Stan Yamagata, our insurance broker, both good friends, not only provide professional services, they also put their hearts into everything they do. Craig Nakamura, of Carlsmith Ball Wichman, and Bruce Noborikawa, of Alston, Hunt, Floyd, & Ing, look out for our legal interests. Lorraine Hamade, a really good friend, has always been our cheerleader. The new wave at Kapalua Land Company—Ed Garces, Kim Carpenter, Scott Crockford, and Carolyn Peters-Egli—continues to support us.

Hawai'i is a small place. We are very fortunate that chefs here join together to share ideas, work together for common causes, and support each other in the true sense of aloha. I am proud to be associated with every single one of them. Chuck Furuya, a good friend, a master sommelier, and more, is a tireless promoter of Hawai'i Regional Cuisine, from the farmers to the culinary programs to all of us chefs—our entire food and beverage industry. He has been a teacher and a leader, providing insightful guidance to many of us. I met Willis Choy in Aspen many moons ago. He and his friends would come to ski (and party!) almost every winter. Those were the good ole days. When I came home, I called on him to help me with a business plan for a restaurant. He agreed without hesitation. To my surprise and great fortune, Willis is one-stop-shopping man! I call him for everything. I trust his business sense and never doubt that he is always looking out for Sansei's and my best interests. He's a true friend.

All Sansei chefs past and present worked on creating the menu that we have today. Current and contributing chefs are corporate chef Tom Selman, executive chefs Ivan Pahk, Keith Endo, and Eric Abrogast, and pastry chef Rodney Weddle.

Our managers run the day-to-day operations of the business. Their tireless effort and drive continuously elevate the business to new heights. Current general managers are Ivy Nagayama, Tom Alejado, and Scott Kodama, and their respective assistants Jason Thompson, Scotty Miyamoto, and Don Bastian. Our bookkeeping staff does a whole lot more than bookkeeping. They run the corporate office and look after the entire staff as if they were their own family members. There is nothing I wouldn't trust our corporate controller,

Sandy Fushikoshi, and staffers Kathleen Kosaka and Jan Beaulieu to handle. Sandy and Kathleen contributed a lot of sweat and tears to this book.

"We're only as good as our last meal" is something our publicist periodically tells us. The restaurant staffs at all three restaurants are really what make Sansei Seafood Restaurant & Sushi Bar so special. I am grateful for their loyalty, conscientiousness, and dedication.

Six years ago, when I first asked for recommendations for a publicist, someone recommended Bonnie Friedman, saying, "She's very expensive, but she's good." So we hired her. We've been working closely together ever since, and she has become part of our family. She works tirelessly to promote Sansei both locally and nationally, she made the deal for this cookbook, and she is my skillful coauthor. She's still expensive . . . but worth every penny.

Thanks to Phil Wood and Jo Ann Deck at Ten Speed Press for their support of this book and their love of Hawai'i and its chefs, to Toni Tajima (a nisei) for designing a beautiful book, and to Kathryn Hashimoto (a sansei) for all her hard work as editor on this project.

When I got married, my father-in-law told me, "No refund!" I was a bit scared at first, but I'm holding him to it, because my wife is the reason I'm part of the Yokoyama family as well as the Kodama family. They treat me like one of their own and are always willing to come out and help when we need them.

Living on the mainland for a lot of years, I missed a lot of holidays and special occasions, not to mention all the regular stuff, with my family. But when I came home and decided to open my own restaurant, they rallied around me 110 percent. They could not be more supportive of Sansei Seafood Restaurant & Sushi Bar and me. I am so grateful to them for coming out to help me at restaurant openings and the many, many promotions and charitable food and wine events. Lucky for me, my family is the epitome of what family is all about. I can call on them for anything, and vice versa. Special thanks to my brothers Greg, Hugh, Scott, and Dennis and their families and my one and only sister, Diane.

Mom and Dad instilled the importance of family and values to us by example. They gave and still give tirelessly without ever asking for anything in return. Mom and Dad are at the restaurant almost every day. I don't pay them, but the only drawback is that I can't fire them! They are not only the best parents in the world, but also the best people I know.

I've saved the best part of me and my thank yous for the two people who mean the most to me. My daughter, Brie Ann, brightens up my day and makes me so happy whenever I look at her. Yes, I am a proud daddy. She is the best daughter that any father could ask for. She is my medicine for a bad day. One look at her, one hug from her, cures all. You know what they say: The fruit doesn't fall far from the tree. My wife, Lori (the tree), is the best thing that ever happened to me. She completes me. She is my confidante, my partner, the one who is not afraid to tell me things I don't want to hear, and my biggest fan. She believes in me and is my greatest supporter. She lets me be me and still wants me. She even laughs at my dry humor. I have balance in my life now. I love you both more and more every day.

To all, I say, "Thank you from the bottom of my heart." There are many, many other people to whom I owe a great deal. There's a saying that goes "How can I soar with eagles, when I'm surrounded by turkeys?" I am so fortunate to always be surrounded by eagles.

Mahalo to each and every one of you.
Domo arigato gozaimashita,
D.K.

Introduction

THIS IS A BOOK about cutting-edge Japanese-inspired Pacific Rim cuisine. It's also a book about family, in the broadest and most embracing sense of that word. It is a book filled with recipes and stories. The force behind the food is a combination of my Japanese heritage, Hawai'i's incredible ethnic mix, and the flavors I've experienced in my travels. The resulting culinary style is unique.

In Hawai'i, there is tremendous importance attached to family. It flows from the native and the Asian traditions—both deeply rooted in these Islands—which often find several generations living under one roof, a roof under which elders are revered. The word *Sansei* itself is a familial reference. It means "third generation," and I am just that: third generation Japanese in Hawai'i. It is in deference to my family traditions that I chose Sansei as the name for my restaurants—with a little help from sister Diane. It's time to finally give credit where credit is due: My sister Diane thought of the name Sansei!

The Kodama Family Comes to Hawai'i

My maternal great-grandfather, Rev. Takie Okumura, came to Honolulu in 1894 as a minister. He was already married to Katsu Ogawa, who joined him two years later. Four of their children were born in Japan; the youngest nine of their thirteen children—including my grandfather, Fuyuki—were born in Hawai'i.

During the outbreak of the black plague in December 1899, the city of Honolulu ordered the home of one of the victims to be burned in an attempt to stem the spread of the disease. The result of that order was the Great Chinatown Fire. And 3,500 Japanese immigrants living in Chinatown at that time lost everything they had. The epidemic and the fire impressed upon my great-grandfather the urgent need for a Japanese hospital. He quickly spearheaded the effort to establish the Japanese Benevolent Hospital in 1900. He was as good a fundraiser as he was a minister. After the United States entered World War II, the name of the hospital was changed to Kuakini Hospital. It eventually grew to become Kuakini Medical Center. Today, it is one of Honolulu's three largest hospitals.

Grandma Tsuwa (my paternal grandmother) came to Hawai'i in 1906 as a "picture bride." Her soon-to-be husband, Grandpa Kamejiro, had arrived from Hiroshima in the great wave of Japanese immigration to Hawai'i at the end of the nineteenth century. He was just sixteen years old. Like most others at that time, he was destined for one of the Islands' sugar plantations, in his case, the one in Pä'ia, Maui. Plantation life, it turned out, was not for him. Just two years after he arrived, he and a partner opened a retail store—which promptly failed. Shortly after his marriage to Grandma, he opened his own business, Kodama's Store, a retail vegetable outlet. This time, he achieved success.

My dad, Tamateru (Tama), was the youngest of four children. As my mom says, "He's typical samurai." He studied civil engineering at the University of Hawai'i from 1947 to 1952. In characteristic steadfast immigrant style, he worked as a licensed civil engineer in the construction industry for fifty years, providing a loving and comfortable home for his family. He retired in 2000. Retired, in Dad's case, is not synonymous with "gone fishing." He helps out at Sansei Seafood Restaurant & Sushi Bar Honolulu almost every day as well as at special events.

My mom, Sandy—aka Mama Kodama, or just Mom—was born in New York City. It was there that her Maui-born mother, Yukie, met her Honolulu-born father, Fuyuki. When Fuyuki's bookstore failed during the depression, Fuyuki and Yukie Okumura brought their young son and daughter back home to Honolulu.

Sandy and Tama were married in 1953 and had six children and now have eight grandchildren. I figure in the middle of the brood; my daughter, Brie Ann, is the youngest of the grandkids.

My mom says that Grandma Tsuwa, who lived with us for twenty-six years, was *the* culinary influence on our family. But there was good cookin' on Mom's side, too. According to Mom, her maternal grandmother was a wonderful cook, with a big copper pot on the stove all day holding stock to which bones were added constantly. Her paternal grandmother ran a cooking school in the late 1890s. It supplemented the family income but was mainly to teach young Japanese women how to make traditional foods, which were unavailable in Hawai'i markets.

As good a cook as Grandma Tsuwa was, though, everyone will tell you my mother is no slouch in the kitchen either. She works in the restaurant almost every single day. By day she's a prep cook, baker, and mom to the entire staff, and by night she is The Hostess with the Mostest. Mom can "work a room" like nobody's business! On Mother's Day 2001, I gave her a chef coat with *Executive Mom* embroidered on it. And on Christmas 2002, her "kids" at the restaurant gave her a spectacular quilt—each square handmade by a staff member. It hangs framed in the Honolulu restaurant dining room.

Mom says that one of the most important things she learned from Grandma Tsuwa was that you must educate your children's palates, and that's what she tried to do with her kids. She believes it's one of the reasons why all six are good cooks.

Following are some recipes from Mom and Grandma Tsuwa, with headnotes written by Mom. These dishes take me back to my childhood, and I remember again the delicious food that was put in front of me with such love and care. Close your eyes and imagine your own mother's or grandmother's kitchen.

Pork and Beans, Kodama-Style

Serves 2

Now it can be told: D.K. was Grandma Kodama's favorite. This was his favorite of her very simple, very American dishes.

1 pound ground beef

1 (24-ounce) can pork and beans

2 tablespoons ketchup

1/2 cup chopped green onion

In a pot over medium heat, stir-fry the beef until browned, about 5 minutes. Add the pork and beans, ketchup, and green onion and simmer over low heat 30 to 45 minutes, until the mixture comes to a low rolling boil. Mix well and serve.

Tuna Patties

Makes 8 patties

When the cupboard is bare, there's no easier meal, especially if you have a house full of hungry kids.

> 2 (6-ounce) cans tuna
>
> 1 small red onion, sliced
>
> 1 egg
>
> 1 tablespoon flour
>
> Salt
>
> 2 tablespoons vegetable oil for frying

In a bowl, combine the tuna, onion, egg, flour, and salt and mix well. Form into 8 patties. In a large skillet, heat the oil over medium heat. In batches, fry the patties for about 2 minutes on each side, until both sides are golden brown. Serve.

Grandma Tsuwa's Ojiya

Serves 4

My mother-in-law's version of seasoned gruel, a family staple in our day. When any of the children showed the first signs of cold or flu, Grandma—and years later, I—would immediately make a batch of ojiya. We used canned clams because they were less expensive than the traditional Japanese hokkigai.

> 3/4 cup short-grain white rice, washed
>
> 1 (15-ounce) can mid-Atlantic cocktail clams with the juice
>
> 1 bunch chives, chopped into 1-inch-long pieces
>
> 2 tablespoons miso
>
> 2 eggs
>
> Salt
>
> Dash of hondashi

In a large pot, bring 8 cups of water to a boil. Add the rice, clams, and clam juice and stir to combine. Decrease the heat to medium. Simmer until the mixture thickens and most of the liquid evaporates, about 30 minutes. Just before removing, add the chives, miso, eggs, salt to taste, and hondashi and stir until combined. Serve.

Fried String Beans

Serves 2

In our home, my husband always wanted a variety of dishes on the table. This was something a little different—and quick and easy—to do with a common vegetable.

1 pound string beans, sliced diagonally into ½-inch pieces
1 tablespoon vegetable oil
Salt
1 egg

Rinse the beans in cold water. Drain, but do not dry. In a frying pan, heat the oil over medium-high heat. When the oil is hot, add the beans to the pan; they should sizzle. Season with salt. Sauté the beans until tender, 2 to 3 minutes. Add the egg to the beans and stir to scramble. Serve.

Grandma Tsuwa's Cabbage Tsukemono (Pickled Cabbage)

Serves 4

Every Japanese family has its own version of this dish. This one comes from my mother-in-law. You must always have pickled cabbage in the house.

1 whole cabbage, quartered
½ cup Hawaiian salt or other coarse salt (enough to make the cabbage squeak)
1 tablespoon sugar
½ cup hot water

In a bowl, sprinkle the cabbage with the salt and sugar. Pour the hot water over the cabbage and cover with a heavy weight. Set aside for half a day. Turn the cabbage over several times after half a day and replace the weight. Let the cabbage soak for 24 hours at room temperature. Rinse the cabbage with fresh water and chop it into bite-size pieces. Serve with soy sauce.

Pickled Cucumbers

Serves 4

When you live in Hawai'i, you need to have a big potluck repertoire. This is a great one because you get a big yield out of a few inexpensive ingredients. It's also a staple of every Japanese home. Kochujang sauce is a Korean seasoning made from miso, honey, and chili pepper. You can buy the bottled sauce in any Asian market.

> 2 cucumbers, sliced into $1/4$-inch-thick rounds
>
> 4 tablespoons sugar
>
> $1/4$ cup vinegar
>
> $1/3$ cup soy sauce
>
> 1 teaspoon Kochujang sauce
>
> 1 teaspoon Asian (toasted) sesame oil
>
> 2 tablespoons toasted sesame seeds

In a bowl, place the cucumbers and sprinkle with 2 tablespoons of the sugar. Set aside. In another bowl, combine the remaining ingredients and mix well. Drain the cucumber, squeezing out any excess liquid. Cover and refrigerate for 24 hours.

Takuwan (Pickled Daikon)

Serves 4

Another staple of every Japanese home. We wouldn't think of going on a picnic or to a potluck without takuwan.

> $1/2$ cup distilled white vinegar
>
> 2 cups sugar
>
> $1/4$ cup salt
>
> $1/4$ teaspoon yellow food coloring
>
> 6 whole daikon, sliced into matchstick-size pieces

In a bowl, combine the vinegar, sugar, salt, and food coloring to make a marinade. In another bowl, combine the daikon with the marinade. Cover and refrigerate for at least 24 hours. It will keep for up to 1 month in the refrigerator.

A *Sansei* Is Born

I was born and raised on Oʻahu in a family pretty typical of second-generation Japanese in Hawaiʻi: hard-working parents and six kids happily living the simple Island life. I was following in my father's footsteps as a civil engineering major at the University of Hawaiʻi and working at a downtown restaurant when the bug bit. I started as a busboy, moved up to server, then bartender. Not only was it fun . . . I got paid, too! *Pau hana* (that's what we call "after work time" here in Hawaiʻi), the guys would get together and fantasize about how cool it would be to own a bar. That fantasy stuck in the back of my mind as a real possibility for me someday.

An opportunity to be a restaurant manager presented itself when friends Robert Peterson, Peter Chalman, and Jim Phelan opened a restaurant in Seattle. It meant moving away from home for the first time, and I accepted. In 1979, I became the first of my clan to venture off to the Mainland . . . and the glamorous restaurant business. I spent three years in Seattle. It was a lot of hard work and very long hours, but I learned *a lot* and really enjoyed it.

The next opportunity came when another friend, Jack Ichikawa, asked me to manage his restaurant in Aspen. I didn't even know where Aspen was, but I jumped at the chance anyway. During my ten years there, I must have worked at twenty different restaurants. I wanted to learn all I could about every aspect of the business. Off-seasons at the ski resort provided me with time to travel throughout the United States, Mexico, and the Caribbean, where my "local boy" palate was introduced to a world of new flavors and culinary styles.

The culinary scene was exploding. Julie Murad-Weiss and Peter O'Grady, who owned Julie & Peter's Creative Catering, taught me classic and contemporary cooking techniques and exposed me to new and exotic products. After that, I worked for Casey Koffman, owner of the famous Takah Sushi Restaurant, who was very patient with me. Lucky for me, because it gave me the opportunity to learn from her amazing head sushi chef, Kenichi Kanada, or "Ken-san."

Well, you can take the local boy out of the Islands but you can't take the Islands out of the local boy, and so I returned to the place I love best. My first job back in Hawai'i was working with Katsuhiko Sato, "Sato-san," at a traditional sushi bar, where he not only refined my skills but also taught me new techniques, introduced me to new items, and explained it all in a way that was easy to understand. He combined patience with skill—the marks of a true mentor.

At about the same time, the Hawai'i Regional Cuisine movement was just starting to gather steam. Local chefs were creating food that was exciting, fresh, beautifully presented, and really tasty. I became inspired and wanted to incorporate some of their wonderfully nontraditional items into my sushi repertoire. I had a sushi bar "concession" at Bev and Joe Gannon's Hali'imaile General Store on Maui, and it was there that I started to experiment with my new-wave sushi. They made great product available to me. I also met Nobu Matsuhisa there, my sushi guru. I was so lucky to work at his side during a special dinner at the General Store and, subsequently, at many other culinary events.

Alice and Dwayne Bower, owners of Le Perle Jewelry Shop in The Shops at Kapalua and longtime customers and friends of mine, told me about a possible site for the sushi bar that we felt ready to open. In March 1996, we opened Sansei the Sushi Bar (later to be renamed Sansei Seafood Restaurant & Sushi Bar) at the old Market Café location. It was a big hit, earning rave reviews and numerous awards. Four years later, I was ready to expand to O'ahu, and our Restaurant Row project opened in April 2000. And I had always wanted to open a second restaurant on the other side of Maui, so with Kapalua doing well and Restaurant Row standing on its own, Sansei Seafood Restaurant & Sushi Bar at Kihei Town Center opened in April 2002.

In August 1999, I became a founding member and one of the first two cochairs of Hawaiian Island Chefs, a nonprofit group dedicated to perpetuating contemporary Island cuisine and to supporting through scholarships the culinary arts programs at all six of Hawai'i's community colleges. That charter membership put me in the company of the so-called next generation of chefs who want to keep the Islands' regional cuisine solidly centered on the global culinary map.

The Boys in the Kitchens

At Sansei Seafood Restaurant & Sushi Bar, each staff member is one of the family. It is a key factor contributing to our success. In order to expand, a restaurateur must have people around him he can trust—with his culinary philosophy, with his image, with his reputation, with his restaurants.

Near the top of the Sansei family tree are the men at the helms of the three Sansei kitchens—Ivan Pahk, Keith Endo, and Tom Selman—each one with a distinct personality and individual style, each a trusted member of the team. In addition to managing a kitchen staff and maintaining the crucially important consistency to the restaurant menus, each is encouraged to infuse his own character and imagination into dishes that become Sansei signatures.

Many of the recipes in this book are the creative contributions of these three talented chefs. The theme of family has not been lost on them, either. They tell me of wonderful childhood culinary memories, of the cooking done by their grandmas and mothers, of their heritages. Stories so warm and comforting, the aromas almost waft out of these pages.

Also invaluable are the contributions of pastry chef Rodney Weddle, who although not technically a family member is certainly a calabash cousin. He contributed most of the dessert recipes in this book. When you try them, you'll understand fully why I always say, "Great things come in 'Weddle' packages!"

CHEF IVAN PAHK

Born and raised on O'ahu's wild North Shore, Ivan Pahk's tender age, diminutive stature, ponytail, jokester-ism, and perfect Pidgin-speak all belie his amazing kitchen skills—with both ingredients and personnel. Blessed with natural talent, sharpened and honed at some of Hawai'i's most noteworthy restaurants, he is as unflappable as he is creative. He is most assuredly my right-hand kitchen man.

Ivan joined Sansei in 1999 as chef of the Kapalua restaurant, where he worked at the shoulder of one of his former mentors. It is a testament to his extreme skill and ingenuity that he was promoted to executive chef one short year later. In February 2002, Ivan returned to his home island to take over as executive chef of Sansei Honolulu. And in October of that same year, he returned to his "adopted" home island of Maui upon his promotion to senior executive chef.

CHEF KEITH ENDO

Born in Southern California, Keith Endo came home to his ancestral Island of Hawai'i when he was a boy. He dreamed of being a CPA (does anyone really dream of being a CPA?) but realized early in his high school career that, as he says, the "numbers thing" just wasn't for him.

If pressed to describe Keith in one word, that word would be "enthusiastic." He is a young chef who loves his work and loves doing that work at Sansei. Keith joined us in 1999 at the Kapalua location and moved to Honolulu shortly thereafter to open the Restaurant Row store. Like most of the senior staffers, he is an integral part of Sansei's growth. He was named executive chef of the Honolulu restaurant in October 2001; in February 2002, he returned to his original Sansei stomping grounds, Kapalua, as executive chef. Several months later, he took back the Honolulu reins from Ivan.

CHEF TOM SELMAN

The culinary elder statesman of the Sansei chefs as well as the newest member of the family, Tom Selman brought with him more than thirty years of experience. The only one of Sansei's senior chefs born and raised on the U.S. Mainland, Tom trained in Florida and Philadelphia with European chefs before moving to Maui in 1997.

He was appointed executive chef of Sansei Kihei several months prior to its April 2002 opening. Six months later, he was promoted to corporate chef with responsibility for all three existing—and all future—restaurants.

PASTRY CHEF RODNEY WEDDLE

A native of Kansas City whose interest in pastry started when he was still in high school, Rodney Weddle truly did find paradise when he came to the Islands in 1986. After working in the pastry kitchens of Hawai'i's best hotels and being at the helm of most of them, in

April 2001 he went out on his own. And now, from his neighborhood pastry kitchen in Honolulu, he creates desserts perfectly suited to Sansei's imaginative cuisine.

What You'll Find in This Book

For lots of folks, Japanese food equals sushi. That word alone is often confusing, even intimidating. Sushi is important enough to be included in the name of our restaurants. So we couldn't even think of doing a cookbook without a substantial sushi chapter. We also include it to prove you don't have to be afraid of it and it doesn't always mean raw fish. Not only that, sushi isn't really all that difficult to make at home, as you'll see when you take my sushi classes at the beginning of this book. It's even easier when you're prepared. That's what *shikomi* means—"to prepare." We've included familiar sushi recipes as well as many of our new-wave specialties.

Having given sushi the credit it's due, I must also say that Japanese food, especially our style of contemporary Japanese food, is about much more than sushi. At Sansei, we offer an extensive list of "small plates." I always encourage our customers to order lots and share, share, share. That way, everyone at the table can enjoy a lot of different flavors. That's what makes a great meal to me. And remember my famous saying: "No wimpy sauces."

Of course, sometimes you just want a nice, big dinner plate with a great piece of fish or meat, rice or potatoes, and vegetables. You'll find plenty of those in our section on "big plates."

I believe that no meal is complete without dessert. Some of our first-time customers are pleasantly surprised at the variety and quality of the desserts we offer. There's no reason for a Japanese dessert to be limited to good ole green tea ice cream. You'll see. . . .

There's a local saying here that goes "Lucky you live Hawai'i." Believe me when I tell you that's an understatement. As chefs and restaurateurs, we have incredible ingredients all around us. As a matter of fact, our local ingredients provide the inspiration for many of our most creative dishes. If you're not lucky enough to live here, have no fear. Wherever you live, there are ingredients you'll be able to use to make the recipes in this book.

There's another "old" saying: "You've come a long way, baby." That's how I feel. I think my grandparents would be very proud that their traditions—their names—are being honored by my generation. It's a privilege to share those traditions, along with new ones created by our Sansei Seafood Restaurant & Sushi Bar family, with all of you.

D.K.'s
Sushi Classes

"Is this microphone on? (tap tap tap) Testing, testing. Ichi, ni, sansei . . .
Sansei Seafood Restaurant and Sushi Bar! That's the name of our restaurant."

That's how I always begin my presentations, cooking demonstrations, classes, or any speaking engagement. The audience usually appreciates my sense of humor. I always try to engage the audience and keep them entertained, whether at a class, at an event, or in one of our dining rooms.

We're going to learn to make sushi, and we'll have fun doing it. In just a few short lessons, you'll be rollin' your own. Here's how we've broken it down: In Sushi 101, you'll learn about ingredients and equipment and basic terminology; in Sushi 201, we'll delve deeper into the different types of sushi and techniques for making them.

First, let's introduce sushi types and the names we use to describe them. Two basic kinds of sushi appear in recipes throughout this book: nigiri and makizushi. Nigiri sushi is made with individual pieces of rice (sushi bars usually serve a pair at a time) topped with a piece of raw fish or other topping; the rice pieces are either molded by hand or shaped in a special nigiri mold. Makizushi is the general name for rolled sushi and refers to a roll of rice, with vegetable and/or protein fillings, wrapped with nori (dried seaweed), then cut into slices. Temaki, or hand rolls, are individual rolled sushi with a small ball of rice and fillings wrapped in nori and shaped into a cylinder or a cone. We'll focus mostly on rolled sushi in these lessons, but we'll also include basic instructions on making nigiri.

Ok, now we can get started. *Ikimashoo!* (Let's go!)

D.K.'s Sushi 101: The Basics

Our syllabus is:

Ingredients: Basic and Advanced

Equipment: Basic and Additional

Extra Credit: Throw a Hand Roll Party for Six!

BASIC INGREDIENTS

I always recommend using the best ingredients you can get. The end product will be tastier and fresher and will look better.

Avocado Haas avocados from California are really the only variety we can recommend. They're sweet, creamy, and great for everything. When shopping for avocados, squeeze them gently. They should be firm but yield to your touch. Overripe avocados will feel mushy.

Crab Mix You can use any type of crabmeat, including imitation crab. Crab is almost always cooked when used in sushi. When shopping for crab, stay away from any that smell like ammonia. Touch it. It should have a clean feel, not slimy. And if you can, taste it—the sweeter, the better. The most important thing about using crab for sushi is to squeeze out all the liquid from the meat. If you don't, it will seep right through the rice and onto the nori, disintegrating it, and the roll will fall apart. Our crab mix recipe is on page 77.

Cucumber Japanese cucumber is best. It's light, crisp, refreshing, doesn't need to be peeled, and has very few, if any, seeds. English, or hothouse, cucumber is a fine substitute. Good old-fashioned American cucumbers should be your last resort—they have a thick, waxy skin that needs to be peeled and lots of seeds that really should be removed. That's too much work.

Gari (Pickled Ginger) At sushi bars, sushi and sashimi are almost always served with pickled ginger on the side.

We've found—and I'm betting most other American sushi bar keepers will tell you the same thing—that the gari never leaves the plate. So what's its purpose? Traditionally, gari is used to cleanse the palate between sushi bites, and should only be eaten one or two small pieces at a time. You can buy it by the jar in any Asian market or the Asian food section of your supermarket.

Kaiware Sprouts These radish (daikon) sprouts have a wonderful, sharp flavor. If you can't find them at your market, try a natural food or gourmet food store.

Nori (Dried Seaweed) You'll find nori packaged in sheets in your supermarket or Asian market. Be sure the package says "yaki-nori," which is precooked and dark green. It should be very dry and shiny, too. Nori is a delicate ingredient and should be kept dry at all times; it's best when fresh and crisp. Want a test for freshness? It should make a lot of noise when you tear it! When you remove the nori from its package, inspect it. One side will be smooth and shiny; the other, dull and rough. In all rolls, the smooth and shiny side should always be outside. Whenever you cut nori, always cut it in half lengthwise. If your nori does become soggy, quickly drag it over an open flame a few times, and it will come back to crispy. Once you open the bag, store the nori in an air-tight container.

Rice The best rice for sushi is short-grain white rice. You should sift through the raw rice and discard any colored or broken grains. Rice is delicate and should not be handled too roughly, whether raw or cooked. When I was growing up, I remember washing the uncooked rice without any particular concern for its delicacy. I'd smash the grains in my clenched fist, believing I was washing it cleaner and faster. Sushi chefs, however, take great pride in their rice and take years to master its cooking. I quickly learned that my washing technique was completely unacceptable. It does make a difference. Rice that is cooked properly will be fluffy and shiny. The recipe for perfect rice is on page 74.

Rice, Sushi Traditionally, sushi rice is called *shari*. It simply means cooked rice that has been "mixed" with shari zu. We explain how to make sushi rice on page 76.

Sesame Seeds (Goma) There are black (kuro) and white (shiro) sesame seeds. We mostly use the white. We use them to coat the outside of our inside-out rolls. Toasting them brings out their flavor. To toast sesame seeds, place them in a dry skillet over medium heat, stirring constantly for about 2 minutes, or until golden brown.

Shari Zu Every sushi chef has his own recipe for shari zu (also called sushi-su), which is a liquid seasoning promptly "cut" into freshly cooked rice to transform rice into sushi rice; you'll find our recipe on page 75. Ideally, every grain of rice should be evenly coated with just enough su. The primary ingredient is rice vinegar, which has a mild, delicate flavor. This is one of those cases when substituting really won't work; most other vinegars are too strong and aromatic.

Shoyu (Japanese Soy Sauce) Shoyu is the Japanese word for soy sauce and is made, obviously, from soybeans. It is used both as a cooking ingredient and as a condiment. You should use Japanese shoyu for sushi, if possible. Once shoyu is opened, it should be kept in a dry, dark, cool place or in the refrigerator.

Tuna Our restaurant has a slogan: "Sansei Seafood Restaurant & Sushi Bar—Home of the Other Red Meat." Tuna is probably the fish most associated with sushi and sashimi. Tuna is to a sushi bar what beef is to a steakhouse. More about tuna coming up in the Advanced Ingredients section.

Tuna, Spicy Spicy tuna is a mixture of chopped tuna, green onion, sesame oil, sambal, cayenne pepper, mayonnaise, and masago. We'll give you the recipe, not to worry (page 78).

Wasabi Wasabi comes in many forms. Fresh wasabi comes from the root of the wasabi plant, which grows in freshwater streams. The root is first peeled and then finely grated. It has a mild bite and is most often compared to horseradish. Fresh wasabi is expensive and not widely available outside of Japan. Frozen wasabi is usually freshly grated and mixed with horseradish before freezing. It's a great substitute for fresh, and it's a lot less expensive. Powdered wasabi is the form most people are familiar with. It's mixed with water to form a thick green paste. Unlike fresh and frozen, the powder is very strong and pungent, with the ability to clear your sinuses! A little goes a long way. Most sushi bars mix the powder with cool water, which enables the paste to last for a few days and keep its potency. At home, it's best to make just what you need for one meal or one party. In the United States, sushi lovers mix wasabi with shoyu and use it as a dipping sauce for sushi and sashimi, something Japanese would never do. Traditionally, wasabi and shoyu are always used separately.

ADVANCED INGREDIENTS

Now that we've got the basic ingredients, we're moving on to the "meat and potatoes," so to speak, of a well-stocked sushi larder. You'll really impress your friends now! First I'll describe the different kinds of neta (sushi toppings), including vegetables and specialty ingredients, then accompaniments.

Talking about neta (sushi toppings) means talking about fish. We're so lucky in Hawai'i to have an abundance of fresh fish readily available to us. There are so many different varieties; it would take a whole other book just to talk about fish, but we'll keep things brief here. First, let's look at how to shop for fish and which fish are commonly used at sushi bars.

Ideally, you want to have your own fishmonger, a knowledgeable person in a fish store with whom you can develop a trusting relationship. Even with a fishmonger's help, though, you should know the basics.

Smell it. It should smell fresh, never "fishy." By fresh I mean a hint of ocean smell. Feel it. It should feel "clean," not slimy. Take a good look at it. The bloodlines should be red, not brown.

When you buy a whole fish, you can't check the flesh. So check the eyes and the gills. The eyes should be clear; the gills should be red. The body should be firm to the touch.

If you buy fish in your supermarket and it's prepacked and covered with plastic wrap, ask an attendant if you can open it to smell it and feel it. If you're told you can't do that, better go someplace else for your fish.

Finally, the shells of every variety of shellfish should be shut tight.

Fish

Now let's look at which fish are commonly used at sushi bars.

Mackerel (Saba) Mackerel has both a strong flavor and a strong aroma. Sushi bars generally pickle their mackerel by salting, rinsing, and marinating it in rice vinegar. Here's how you do it. First, gently rub the mackerel fillet with sea salt and let sit in a colander over a plate large enough to catch the dripping juices for 30 minutes to 1 hour; rinse well with water to completely remove the salt and pat dry. Transfer the mackerel to a shallow dish and marinate in rice vinegar for 1 to 2 hours; the flesh will turn white. The end result is one of my favorite flavors because of the abundance of abura (omega-3 fatty acids). Saba will differ from sushi bar to sushi bar, sushi chef to sushi chef, and it is used as a measure of a great sushi chef or a great sushi bar.

Salmon (Sake), Smoked Salmon (Sake) Salmon is one of my favorite nigiri sushi. I usually order salmon with shiso and saba with shiso. Salmon should never be served raw, fresh out of the water. It should always be smoked, cured, or cooked. The curing process we use involves salting the fish (to extract the liquids and rid it of its smell), rinsing, and then freezing to kill any parasites. Salmon's naturally vibrant orange color and sweet taste make it a sushi party favorite. And it's available just about everywhere.

Snapper (Tai) In Japan, tai is sea bream, a species of fish that stays fresh for a long time. Because sea bream is not widely available in the United States, sushi bars use many other varieties of fish for tai. Red snapper tastes similar to sea bream, and it is the most widely used fish to replace tai.

Tuna (Maguro) Here in Hawai'i, we see mainly yellowfin in the summer, bigeye in the winter, and bluefin mostly in the winter and mostly from the northeast coast of the Mainland. Ahi traditionally refers to bigeye and yellowfin caught in Hawaiian waters. There are several terms to describe the various cuts of tuna: otoro (very fatty tuna), toro (fatty tuna), chutoro (half fatty, half red tuna), and akami (red tuna). Otoro usually comes from bluefin. The fattier the tuna, the better. Otoro is the fattiest cut of all tuna. Like Barbra Streisand says, "It's like buttah." Because it's the most prized tuna, tastes awesome, and comes from fish found only in extremely cold waters, otoro is very expensive and not readily available. The next fattiest is toro, then chutoro, and finally akami, which is a lean, red tuna.

Chutoro and akami, which come from the entire loin of the fish, are graded for quality based on smell, texture, and visual appeal. The finest grade is called #1 or sushi/sashimi (or Tokyo) quality, followed by A, B, C, and, finally, cooking tuna. Otoro and toro always come from the belly section and are not graded.

If you had these four types lined up side by side, the otoro would be the lightest pink with lots of marbling, toro would be pink, chutoro would be half pink and half red, and grade A akami would be the reddest in color. Likewise, if you did a taste test with these same four, the otoro would be the most buttery and tender, while the akami would be the leanest and the "cleanest." The best toro, chutoro, and otoro come from blue fin.

Yellowtail (Hamachi) Yellowtail is a variety of tuna. In sushi bars, yellowtail is more commonly referred to as hamachi, which is a young yellowtail. Mature yellowtail is called buri. Hamachi is light coral in color, not red like ahi. Hamachi is rich with a slightly smoky taste. Hamachi may not always be available in sushi bars or supermarkets, so it's a treat when you do find it. Many people also enjoy eating the shoulder (kama) that has been broiled, grilled, or fried.

Shellfish

The following shellfish are commonly found at sushi bars.

Clams There are so many varieties of clams, but the one you will most commonly see at the sushi bar is mirugai (geoduck clam), which is usually served live and raw. It should be hard but crunchy, and should move when you touch it or drip lemon juice on it. The best mirugai is grade A; it's white, clean, and sweet. The lower grades will be brown to dark brown in color and have a muddier flavor. Other varieties, which are usually frozen, are hokkigai (surf clam), akagai (red clam), and torigai (bird clam).

Oysters (Kaki) Just like their clam cousins, there are many varieties of oysters. Oysters used to be seasonal, but many varieties are now farm raised, so they're available year-round. But it also means we are at the mercy of the oyster "farmers" in terms of available varieties. The best oysters, no matter which variety, should always be live in their shells, plump, and pearl-colored with tinges of gray.

Scallops (Hotategai, Kaibashira) Most sushi bars use frozen scallops. Very few use fresh, which are known as day boat scallops (these are sea scallops that we get the day they come off the boat). Fresh scallops have a very short shelf life and can spoil easily. With modern technology, the best scallops that we've come across are frozen and vacuum-packed. In general, the smaller ones are called bay scallops and the larger ones are called sea scallops. Make sure that the scallops you are getting have not been soaked in chemicals (which act as a preservative and also alter size and color); chemical-free scallops are sometimes called "dry pack" scallops. Before using, be sure to remove the hinge muscle on the side.

Shrimp (Ebi) Jumbo shrimp, or prawns, are very popular at sushi bars, especially with those who are squeamish about eating raw fish. Ebi is the most common sushi topping and is served cooked.

Sweet Shrimp (Amaebi) Amaebi is a specialty item and definitely an acquired taste. The tail is usually served raw—it's sweet and has a pasty texture that some folks just don't like. The head is fried crispy and served either with a dipping sauce or plain salt. Yes, folks, you eat it whole. Try the crispy legs first; the texture is like eating a shrimp chip.

Other Seafood

And here are other creatures from the sea used to top sushi.

Abalone (Awabi) Awabi can be served raw only if it is still alive. Press your finger on the awabi. If it moves, it's still alive. The firmer awabi, the male, is preferable for sushi.

Eel, Freshwater (Unagi) Unagi is very popular in American sushi bars. Maybe one of the reasons is that it's never served raw. It's usually grilled and glazed with tare (a sweet, soy-based sauce). It tastes like smoky teriyaki. Unagi is available at supermarkets already cooked and glazed. All you need to do is open the package, heat, and serve. Because it already has a soy-based flavoring, you don't even need a dipping sauce. What could be easier? To heat the unagi, place under a preheated broiler for 2 minutes, until heated through.

Eel, Saltwater (Anago) The preparation of anago is a barometer for measuring a sushi chef's skill. It's the only type of eel served at traditional sushi bars. In Japan, the first items a serious sushi eater will order are anago, tamago (egg), and saba (mackerel). If they're good, then he will stay. If not, he will leave, sometimes not even paying his tab. The stock in which the anago is boiled is used afterward as the base for both anago and unagi (freshwater eel) glazes.

Flying Fish Roe (Tobiko) Tobiko is about the same size as masago (smelt roe) but is closer in taste to caviar—crunchy and salty. Tobiko is also used as a topping for nigiri sushi. The best thing about tobiko is that you can save some for later. They always find a way of hiding way, way back in your mouth, and when you least expect it—crunch!

Octopus (Tako) When buying tako that is already cooked, it's difficult to determine how fresh it is. Look for tako that does not have any broken skin or black spots and skin that does not tear easily when pulled. Because of its chewy texture, tako is usually boiled, chilled, then sliced for sashimi and sushi. My daughter's first taste of table food was tako, because it's a natural teething aid. She loved it!

Salmon Roe (Ikura) Ikura is the most popular roe in sushi bars. Better sushi bars will wash the roe, then marinate it in a soy-mirin–based dashi (Japanese soup stock); our marinade recipe is on page 79. It's a fun food for me. I like the feel of them eggs squishin' in my mouth. Ikura look like tiny red water balloons the size of peas.

Sea Urchin (Uni) Uni is an expensive delicacy. Sea urchins are small, prickly, porcupine-looking creatures. Once the spikes and the body are removed, what's left in the shell is uni. If you want to get technical, it's actually the gonads. It's sort of mustard brown in color and has a very distinct nutty flavor. If it's good, it's really good. If it's bad, it's really bad. It should be sweet and creamy, with an avocado-like texture.

Smelt Roe (Masago) Masago is small orange smelt roe. It has a crunchy texture and slightly sweet taste. Masago is a common topping for nigiri sushi. It's also a colorful way to garnish the rice on an inside-out roll and is great in sauces. Masago is available in the frozen food section of Asian markets.

Spicy Cod Roe (Mentaiko) Mentaiko is salted for preservation and spiced with Korean chili pepper. There are many different ways to eat mentaiko. One of the most common is to throw mentaiko on a flame, sear the outside, and eat it with rice and pickles. It can also be eaten in a roll with cucumber and shiso (perilla leaf) and used as a topping for nigiri sushi.

Squid (Ika) Ika can be served either raw or grilled. Usually the body is sliced, scored, and served raw, and the geso (tentacles) are grilled and served with a sweet teriyaki-style glaze.

Vegetables

Now let's discuss the variety of vegetables that are used in or alongside sushi.

Burdock (Gobo) Gobo is a long, slender root vegetable. It has a texture similar to carrots. If you find it at a sushi bar, it will likely be pickled. In restaurants, it's usually cooked with shoyu, mirin, and sugar, and the resulting dish is called kinpira gobo. It can be found, pickled or fresh, at Asian markets.

Carrot (Ninjin) Carrots are often used as a garnish or a condiment.

Citrus Limes, lemons, and oranges are used in seasonings and to garnish many dishes. Yuzu (citron) is a Japanese citrus fruit with a sour taste; it's difficult to find fresh, but bottled yuzu juice is available in Asian markets.

Daikon, Pickled (Takuan) Depending on the coloring agent, this radish can be pale yellow or brown. Depending on the particular preparation, the taste can be sweet and/or salty.

Edamame (Green Soybeans) Japanese amuse-bouche. Fresh soybeans are lightly boiled, drained, and lightly salted. Eat only the beans, throw the shell away. We new-wave chefs use edamame as we would any beans: in hummus; instead of mashed potatoes as the starch that accompanies an entrée; whole in salads or succotash.

Green Onion (Negi) Be sure to slice green onions very, very thin, using only the green parts. Place the slices in a fine-mesh colander or strainer with a bowl underneath and wash off the bitter, green, slimy innards under running water. Then dry the slices. You will end up with beautiful, thin green onion "rings" that are not bitter, but still sharp. They add a great flavor to lots of dishes.

Kampyo (Seasoned Gourd) Kampyo is dried strips of gourd "meat." They have a natural color and should not be brown or white. Kampyo is boiled and then cooked in a shoyu-sugar-mirin seasoning. Once cooked, it has a transparent, rubbery look and feel, but it tastes good. Kids love it in a roll. It's available at some Asian markets precooked, but it's much better if you prepare it at home: First, boil the long strips of dried kampyo until tender, about 5 minutes, then poach in a mixture of 1 part mirin, 1 part sugar, and $1/2$ part shoyu for about 5 minutes, until soft. Let cool before using.

Konbu (Kelp) Konbu is dried kelp or seaweed. It comes in dried black sheets with a white powdery film on it. The powder should be wiped off, but not rinsed. Konbu is used to flavor soup stocks and shari zu. It's also available in Asian markets in wide and thin strips, and some are even precut into small (about 1-inch-square) pieces.

Mesclun (Mixed Salad Greens) It's always good to have some farm-fresh, exotic greens on hand. They make great salads, of course, but they're also a nice garnish, like around our Mango and Crab Salad Hand Roll (page 104).

Mountain Yam (Yamaimo) Yamaimo is a root vegetable, brown on the outside and creamy white on the inside. When it's grated, the end product is a creamy, white, gooey substance just like a raw beaten egg. Whether sliced, diced, or chunked, it still has an okralike texture, although cleaner and crisper. No matter what you do to it, yamaimo has very little flavor, so you'll want to add shoyu and wasabi.

Shiso (Perilla or Beefsteak Leaf) Shiso, as in "she's so fine." (I used that line a lot when my wife used to assist me at cooking demonstrations.) I love shiso. I love its distinct, sharp, herby flavor. It can be used as an herb, a garnish, or a condiment. Shiso is part of the mint family and looks very much like mint.

Tsuma Tsuma is not really a vegetable; it's a style of cutting that is used as a garnish or as a condiment with sashimi. Tsuma can be made with daikon, carrots, beets, cucumber—any vegetable. The vegetables are cut into long, fine curly threads. It can be done by hand, or you can make your life easy with a contraption made by Benriner for just this purpose.

Ume (Sour Plum) Ume is a red sour-salty plum that goes well with rice, which is why it's used in rolls, mainly in a seedless, paste form. You'll see a lot of seasoned sushi eaters finish off a meal with ume shisomaki (sour plum roll), as they believe it helps with digestion. Ume is readily available in the Asian section of supermarkets.

Wakame (Seaweed) There are, literally, dozens and dozens of different seaweeds. This is the one used in miso soup and salads. It usually comes dried and needs to be reconstituted by soaking it in warm water. The texture is smooth, like noodles.

Specialty Ingredients

Now here are some additional specialty ingredients. We're getting really fancy now. Just try to imagine how impressed your friends are going to be!

Furikake (Rice Seasoning) We use furikake to coat the rice on our inside-out rolls. It's also a great thing to sprinkle on kids' rice. Furikake is available in Asian markets, with lots of different mixes to choose from; the specific ingredients vary, but basically it consists of sesame seeds, dried seaweed, dried fish, and salt.

Mamenori (Soybean Wrappers) Mamenori are thin, pliable sheets made of soy. They come in really cool colors: neon pink, green, and yellow. We use this to make sushi for guests who are allergic to or don't care for nori—or if we just want a roll to look particularly hip! Several upscale Asian markets in Hawai'i carry mamenori, a few of the major Japanese supermarkets on the Mainland will have it, or you can order it online from an Asian or sushi food supplier.

Natto (Fermented Soybeans) You'll either love natto or . . . not. It's got a flavor—and smell—all its own. You need to decide to ignore the smell and its ooey-gooey texture, otherwise you won't even try it. I predict that if you do, you will love it! It's often eaten with shoyu over rice. It's one of my personal favorites!

Pickled Vegetables (Oshinko) The pickling can be done using lots of different veggies. Pickled vegetables work as a side dish and a sushi filling.

Quail Egg (Uzura) This is *way* more expensive per egg than chicken eggs *and* a tiny fraction of the size. Go figure! Quail eggs are usually eaten raw atop other "eggs" such as tobiko and uni.

Sambal (Indonesian Chili Paste) This has a great taste and is not as hot as chili peppers.

Sesame Oil Sesame oil is a distinctive nutty seasoning. We use it in our spicy tuna, among many other dishes. Be sure to use the darker-colored, more fragrant seasoning oil rather than the lighter-colored cooking oil.

Tamago (Egg Omelet) One of the three types of sushi (along with anago and saba) used to measure a sushi chef's skill. Making tamago properly is not easy. It takes a lot of patience and practice. Tamago is on the sweet side, and it can be eaten at the beginning or at the end of a meal. Our tamago recipe is on page 80.

Tofu "Tofu is great. It takes on whatever flavor you cook it with." I once did a commercial promoting tofu, and that was my line. Actually, it's true. Tofu is so versatile: It can be eaten plain, with shoyu, or cooked in stir-fries such as chicken tofu, or even fried. And it's so healthy.

Accompaniments

The following ingredients we can classify as sushi accompaniments.

Fish Sauce This juice of salted fish is essential to Southeast Asian cooking. With a range in flavor and coloring, each country has its own version. It's available in Asian markets as nam pla from Thailand, nuoc nam from Vietnam, and patis from the Philippines, among others; we like to use patis in our recipes.

Katsuobushi (Bonito Flakes) These are just what you'd expect—thin, dried shavings of dried bonito. Bonito is one of the main ingredients in dashi (Japanese soup stock). It's also used as an accompaniment to dishes like hiyayakko (chilled tofu).

Mirin (Sweet Rice Wine) Mirin is used in cooking as a sweetener. Most of the alcohol content usually cooks off.

Momiji Oroshi (Grated Daikon with Chili Peppers) Momiji oroshi is a condiment for sauces and is most commonly used in ponzu sauce. It's easy to make: just grate daikon radish and add a pinch of cayenne pepper, or to your taste.

Panko (Japanese Breadcrumbs) Panko is used in Japanese cooking to coat fried food. It's lighter and flakier than other types of breadcrumbs and makes a light, crispy crust.

Ponzu (Citrus Soy Sauce) Ponzu is made with yuzu (citron) juice and shoyu. It's usually served with sashimi. You can find it at Asian markets. (Some products refer to the yuzu juice alone as ponzu.)

Rice Vinegar This mild, low-acid vinegar is a must-have in every Japanese pantry. And be sure to get Japanese rather than Chinese rice vinegar. It's a bit less acidic and a little sweeter than its Chinese cousin.

Sake (Rice Wine) Ah! We use sake in a lot of sauces—and to take the edge off a bad day. Although its spelling is the same as the Japanese word for salmon, there is a slight difference in pronunciation.

Sansho It's just Japanese pepper. Sansho is often sprinkled over anago.

Shichimi (Seven-Spice Pepper) Made up of red pepper flakes, dried orange peel, green nori, sansho, black hemp seeds, white poppy seeds, and black sesame seeds, this Japanese spice combo is so *ono* (delicious)! It's available in Asian markets.

Tempura Batter Tempura batter is simply a mixture of eggs, flour, and ice water. In recipes that call for it, use the prepared dry mix (just add water) available in Asian markets.

Yuzu (Japanese Citrus) Yuzu has a unique aroma and flavor. We use it to flavor sauces and to season dishes.

BASIC EQUIPMENT ("SORTA GOTTA HAVES")

While not essential (you can usually find something in your kitchen that will work), having the proper equipment will make the job a lot easier. Because we live in such a multicultural community here in Hawai'i, many homes already have most of the basics. You probably do, too. If you don't and you want to invest in some equipment, the following will help you sift through what you really need.

Bamboo Mat (Maki Su) A maki su is made by tying bamboo sticks together with cotton string to form a mat. It's used to roll makizushi and to shape uramaki rolls. It's a very cool, very inexpensive tool. After washing, be sure to dry it completely before storing.

Cutting Board This is essential. Sushi—and all Japanese food, for that matter—involves a lot of prep. Every single ingredient will be cut, in one form or another. If you plan to cut fish often, it's a good idea to dedicate one side of the board, or a separate cutting board altogether, to fish.

A Good, Sharp Knife Chefs, including sushi chefs, always work with a variety of good knives. For home use, you only need one. A 10- or 12-inch chef's knife is all-purpose. Most important is that you keep it sharp; sushi must be cleanly cut. Also, when cutting sushi, the knife blade should be kept moist, not wet, at all times.

Rice Cooker Every single home in Hawai'i has at least one rice cooker. Some people even take them along on vacation. And no local kid would leave for school or work on the Mainland without his or her rice cooker. Rice cookers make cooking rice so easy. They automatically regulate the heat and time for cooking. If you cook rice on any regular basis, I encourage you to buy one; they're not expensive. I promise you will fall in love.

Rice Paddle (Shamoji) Rice paddles are used to "cut" and serve rice. Another very small investment for something guaranteed to become one of your favorite utensils. Wooden ones absorb flavors, so if you choose wood, always keep one for rice only. Plastic ones are just fine. Remember to wet your rice paddle before using, so the rice won't stick to it.

Rice Tub (Hangiri) A hangiri is a square, shallow wooden tub used to cool the rice and to "cut" the su into the rice. If you don't have a hangiri, then a wooden bowl—or any container other than a stainless steel bowl—will do.

Vegetable Peeler This is essential—unless, of course, you enjoy peeling vegetables with a knife.

ADDITIONAL EQUIPMENT ("GOOD TO HAVES")

The following tools will help you achieve near-professional presentations and will definitely impress your friends. You might want to purchase these to get you to the "head of the class."

Bamboo Skewers Skewering shrimp is the best way to keep them from curling while cooking.

Colander To wash rice and wash and drain other ingredients. I'm guessing everyone has one.

Cooking Chopsticks (Saibashi) Cooking chopsticks are much longer and usually thicker than eating chopsticks and are very useful for reaching into deep pots or pans on the back burners of the stove.

Fish Scaler Go against the grain of the scales, and work from tail to head to remove fish scales. A knife works, too.

Grater Have on hand any kind—box grater, flat grater—for vegetables.

Mandoline A mandoline is a very cool tool. Basically, it's a slicer. You can slice from thick to extremely thin; it's great for making pickled vegetables. There are plastic ones and stainless steel ones, and they vary greatly in price.

Nigiri Mold Nigiri is fish on top of sushi rice, and the rice is always molded—either by hand or, much more easily, in a nigiri mold. Nigiri molds come in all shapes—rectangular is most common. Nigiri molds are made of wood or plastic and can be purchased at any Asian market.

Omelet Pan and Wooden Geta A very helpful tool found in Japanese markets for making tamago. A traditional Japanese omelet pan is square. A wooden geta fits in the pan and helps to form the omelet. You can use a round pan, and then cut the round omelet into a square or fold in the sides to form a square. But you'll never see a round pan in a sushi bar. You know the old saying about a round peg in a square hole. . . .

Rice Holder This should be an insulated container used to hold your sushi rice during service. A cooler will work just fine.

Scissors Any sharp pair will do. Use them to cut nori and other ingredients. Again, a pair should be reserved for this purpose and should live in the kitchen rather than the sewing box.

Squirt Bottles You know, like the ones you use for mustard and ketchup at picnics. They're inexpensive and the best way to "paint" plates. Your friends will be so impressed!

Toaster Oven That's right, a toaster oven. No sushi bar would be caught without one. We use it to broil fish and specialty dishes.

Turning Slicer I think cutting by hand produces a better quality product, but this tool makes cutting long, thin strings of vegetables, usually root vegetables, fast and easy. You can cut from extremely thin to wide.

Tweezers Tweezers are used to remove small bones from fish. Please use one purchased at a fish market specifically for this purpose, not the one you use on your eyebrows. Small jewelry pliers with a sharp nose will work too, but again, please reserve it for this purpose.

EXTRA CREDIT: THROW A HAND ROLL PARTY FOR SIX!

Okay, it's time to put our money where our mouth is! Let's make some temaki (hand rolls). It will take practice to get it right. Please don't get frustrated. Just eat all the mistakes and use the shoyu and wasabi as dipping sauces. As far as ingredients go, these are the basic components of sushi: sushi rice, filling, nori, shoyu, wasabi, and gari. Beyond these, your only limit will be your imagination. You can use anything that goes with rice—which is just about everything—like teriyaki chicken, seared foie gras, natto, or steak. Always make sure there's enough of everything for everyone; that's the local way. Use the quantities we've given you only as guidelines. Let's get ready. . . .

Here's our basic menu:

6 Tuna Hand Rolls	*3 Crab Tuna Hand Rolls*
6 California Hand Rolls	*3 Vegetarian Hand Rolls*
6 Spicy Tuna Hand Rolls	

Here's the basic equipment to have on hand:

Knife   *Rice paddle*

Cutting board   *Bowls*

Rice cooker   *Spoons*

Rice tub (hangiri)   *Towels*

You'll need these ingredients:

12 cups Sushi Rice (page 76)   *15 whole sheets nori (dried seaweed)*

3 cups Crab Mix (page 77)   *3 tablespoons white sesame seeds,toasted (page 16)*

3 cups Spicy Tuna Mix (page 78)

1 pound sashimi-grade tuna   *1/2 cup powdered wasabi*

4 Japanese cucumbers   *1 cup shoyu (Japanese soy sauce)*

2 haas avocados   *1/2 cup gari (pickled ginger)*

Prepare the sushi rice, crab mix, and spicy tuna mix. Transfer into separate bowls and cover tightly. Refrigerate the crab mix and spicy tuna mix until ready to use.

Cut the tuna into long strips or chop it. Place in an airtight container and refrigerate until ready to use. Slice the cucumbers lengthwise into sticks, about as wide as a pencil and about 4 inches long. Cut the avocados in half. Remove the pit from each and slice lengthwise into 1/4-inch-thick slices. Cut each sheet of nori in half lengthwise.

Transfer the toasted sesame seeds to a shaker or a bowl with a spoon. Mix the wasabi with water, forming a soft paste that can be easily diluted in shoyu. Transfer the shoyu to a serving container with a spout. Put the gari in a bowl.

Place all the ingredients on the serving table with appropriate serving utensils.

Now you're ready to learn the techniques. There are two types of temaki (hand rolls). One is cylindrical and holds solid ingredients, for example, a tuna roll. The other is conical (looks like an ice cream cone) and is used to keep smaller ingredients, like salmon roe, from seeping through the bottom. When handling the rice, be sure to slightly wet your hands first by dipping them in a bowl filled with water and a little rice vinegar, to keep the rice from sticking to your hands—but don't overdo it, or the rice will get soaked.

Basic Technique for Cylindrical Rolls

Place the nori shiny-side down in the palm of your hand, with the shorter side perpendicular to your fingers. With your other hand, pick up a golf ball–size portion of rice and spread it evenly on the third of the nori closest to your thumb. With your finger or the back of a spoon, rub $1/2$ teaspoon of wasabi (more or less, depending on your taste and tolerance for heat) on the rice. Sprinkle on a light, even layer of sesame seeds, then stack the desired filling on top. Using your free hand, roll the nori into a cylindrical shape.

Basic Technique for Conical Rolls

Place the nori shiny-side down diagonally in the palm of your hand. With your other hand, pick up a golf ball–size portion of rice and spread it evenly on the third of the nori closest to your thumb. With your finger or the back of a spoon, rub $1/2$ teaspoon of wasabi (more or less, depending on your taste and tolerance for heat) on the rice. Sprinkle on a light, even layer of sesame seeds, then stack the desired filling on top. Using your free hand, fold the bottom corner of nori furthest from you over the filling and shape into a cone.

A Note about Nigiri

At sushi bars, the individual rice pieces used in nigiri are formed by hand, and it can be a difficult technique to master. Instead, you might want to purchase a nigiri mold, which forms the rice pieces quickly and easily. To form the pieces by hand, scoop a small handful of rice in one hand (remember to keep the hands slightly wet when handling rice) and use the other hand to help shape the rice into a rectangle. To finish the nigiri, take a slice of fish and smear a little wasabi on its underside, then lightly press the rice piece onto the slice; the topping should completely cover the top of the rice.

So you've got the ingredients, you know the techniques . . . it's time to party! Just add some tuna to make a tuna hand roll or some spicy tuna mix to make a spicy tuna roll. To assemble a California roll, add crab mix along with cucumber and avocado before rolling. To make a crab tuna hand roll, combine the crab mix with tuna (or the spicy tuna mix, if you prefer). Use the vegetable slices to make either a cucumber hand roll or a cucumber avocado hand roll. Or mix and match as you wish.

Let everyone make their own hand rolls, both cylindrical and conical, and discover how much fun you can have playing with your food. If extra rice and tuna slices are on hand, practice making nigiri sushi. The more you practice, the easier it will get. By the end, you'll be making plans for the next party and everyone will want to create even more rolled sushi. That's where the next class comes in. . . .

D.K.'s Sushi 201: Makizushi

Prerequisite: Successful completion of D.K.'s Sushi 101
Our syllabus is:

Types of Makizushi and Techniques

Temaki	*Hosomaki*
Tatemaki	*Futomaki*
Horizontal Uramaki	*Vertical Uramaki*

TYPES OF MAKIZUSHI AND TECHNIQUES

Makizushi is to Japanese what a sandwich is to Americans—both are portable and can be eaten with one hand. Many people are introduced to sushi with makizushi. For first-time sushi eaters who are squeamish about eating anything raw, makizushi is the way to go. There are many rolls that are not made with any raw fish or seafood. A good roll for beginners is any roll with the rice on the outside (uramaki), so the first taste is rice, not nori. Nori has a strong ocean flavor that is enjoyed by sushi aficionados but can turn off a novice. Going even one step further, for those who find the taste of nori too strong, at Sansei we use mamenori, or soybean wrap, in place of the nori. Mamenori has a very mild flavor.

Many customers have walked into the restaurants saying they don't eat sushi but were forced to come because they were outnumbered by sushi lovers. We make sure those folks leave happy, having enjoyed everything, including the sushi. We aim to please and can accommodate everyone. Everything at a sushi bar need not be raw . . . except maybe the cucumbers.

Temaki (Hand rolls)

To review this technique, please go back to the party (page 30)!

Hosomaki (Long, thin rolls with 1 or 2 fillings)

On a bamboo mat, right along its lower edge, place the nori, shiny-side down and with the long side closest to you. Spread the sushi rice evenly on the nori, leaving a $1/2$-inch border across the top. Using your finger, spread the wasabi paste and other spreads evenly across the middle of the rice. Place the fillings in the middle of the rice. With your thumbs, lift the edge of the mat that's closest to you. Using your fingers to keep the filling in place, roll the edge of the nori away from you so that it just slightly tucks under the filling. Continue to roll the nori, jelly-roll style, into a tight cylinder, removing the mat as you go. The ideal diameter for this type of roll is about 1 inch. The seam should be on the bottom. Make sure that the ends are tucked in so the roll doesn't fall apart when you cut it. Using a sharp knife, cut crosswise into 6 equal pieces, about 3/4 inch thick.

HOSOMAKI EXAMPLE: Asparagus Roll

Makes 1 roll

Fresh springtime asparagus with its earthy tones is the perfect match for the sushi rice and the nori. It's so simple and so delicious.

Cottonseed, peanut, or canola oil, for deep-frying

3 long, thin spears asparagus

1/2 sheet, cut lengthwise, nori (dried seaweed)

1 cup Sushi Rice (page 76)

Wasabi paste

1 teaspoon Masago Aioli (page 76)

To prepare the asparagus, in a heavy saucepan, pour in the oil to a depth of 3 inches and heat to 375°. Add the asparagus to the oil and quick-fry, turning with tongs to cook evenly for about 1 minute, until golden brown. Using a slotted spoon, transfer the asparagus to paper towels to drain.

To assemble, place the nori shiny-side down on a bamboo mat with the long side closest to you. Spread the rice evenly on the nori, leaving a 1/2-inch border across the top. Spread the wasabi across the middle of the rice. Spread the masago aioli alongside the wasabi. Place the asparagus evenly on top of the wasabi and aioli. Complete the roll, following the technique to make hosomaki. Cut into 6 pieces. Serve with shoyu, wasabi, and gari.

Tatemaki (Short, "fat" rolls with as many fillings as you want)

On a bamboo mat, right along its lower edge, place the nori, shiny-side down and with the short side closest to you. Spread the sushi rice evenly on the nori, leaving a 1-inch border across the top. If the recipe calls for sesame seeds, sprinkle over the rice. Using your finger, spread the wasabi paste or other spreads evenly across the rice, about one-third of the way from the bottom. Place the fillings evenly across the bottom one-third of the rice. With your thumbs, lift the edge of the mat that's closest to you. Using your fingers to keep the filling in place, roll the edge of the nori away from you so that it just slightly tucks under the filling. Continue to roll the nori, jelly-roll style, into a tight cylinder, removing the mat as you go. The seam should be on the bottom. Make sure that the ends are tucked in so the roll doesn't fall apart when you cut it. Using a sharp knife, cut crosswise into 6 equal pieces.

TATEMAKI EXAMPLE: Spicy Tuna Roll

Makes 1 roll

The problem I've always had with spicy tuna rolls is that they're spicy but not tasty. Ours is unique because it's as flavorful as it is spicy. We achieve that through the use of a little sesame oil for nuttiness, masago for sweetness, and aioli for creaminess—all these in the spicy tuna mix.

> $^1/_2$ sheet, cut lengthwise, nori (dried seaweed)
> 1 cup Sushi Rice (page 76)
> 1 teaspoon white sesame seeds, toasted (page 16)
> 3 tablespoons Spicy Tuna Mix (page 78)
> 2 ($^1/_4$ by 4-inch) sticks Japanese cucumber

To assemble, place the nori shiny-side down on a bamboo mat with the short side closest to you. Spread the rice evenly on the nori, leaving a 1-inch border across the top. Sprinkle with the sesame seeds. Spread the spicy tuna mix across the bottom third of the rice. Stack the cucumber sticks end to end on the tuna. Use the bamboo mat to complete the roll, following the technique to make tatemaki. Cut into 6 pieces. Serve with shoyu, wasabi, and gari.

Futomaki (It means "big roll")

Use a whole sheet of nori. On a bamboo mat, right along its lower edge, place the nori, shiny-side down. Spread the sushi rice evenly on the nori, leaving a 1-inch border across the top. If the recipe calls for wasabi paste, spread it evenly across the middle portion of the rice. Arrange the fillings on top. With your thumbs, lift the edge of the mat that's closest to you. Using your fingers to keep the filling in place, roll the nori away from you so that it just slightly tucks under the filling. Continue to roll the nori, jelly-roll style, into a tight cylinder, removing the mat as you go. The seam should be on the bottom. Make sure that the ends are tucked in so the roll doesn't fall apart when you cut it. Using a sharp knife, cut crosswise into 8 equal pieces.

FUTOMAKI EXAMPLE: Spider Roll

Makes 1 roll

This roll is named after the way it looks. If you do it right, it looks like spider legs are coming out of the roll. If you can't see it, have another sake and beer, and look again.

Cottonseed, peanut, or canola oil, for deep-frying
2 soft-shell crabs
$1/2$ cup cornstarch
1 sheet nori (dried seaweed)
2 cups Sushi Rice (page 76)
3 tablespoons Masago Aioli (page 76)
2 ($1/4$ by 5-inch) sticks Japanese cucumber
1 tablespoon gari (pickled ginger)
2 pieces pickled burdock (gobo)
$1/3$ cup kaiware sprouts
1 teaspoon thinly sliced green onion, green part only, for garnish

To prepare the crab, in a heavy saucepan, pour in the oil to a depth of 3 inches and heat to 360°. Turn the crabs in the cornstarch until coated evenly. Add the crabs to the oil and fry for about 5 minutes, until very crisp. Using a slotted spoon, transfer the crabs to paper towels to drain.

To assemble the roll, place the nori shiny-side down on a bamboo mat. Spread the rice evenly on the nori, leaving a 1-inch border across the top. Spread the masago aioli across the bottom third of the rice. Place the crabs, side by side, on top of the masago aioli, with the legs sticking out on both sides. On top of the crab, stack the cucumber, gari, gobo, and kaiware sprouts, positioning the leaf ends of the sprouts towards the outer edges of the roll. Use the bamboo mat to complete the roll, following the technique to make futomaki. Cut into 6 pieces. Sprinkle the green onion on top. Serve with momiji oroshi and ponzu sauce.

Horizontal Uramaki (Inside-out hosomaki)

On a clean, dry cutting board, place the nori, shiny-side down and with the long side closest to you. Spread the rice evenly to cover the entire nori. If the recipe call for sesame seeds, sprinkle over the rice. Flip the nori over so the rice side is facing down and the nori side is facing up. With the long side still closest to you, arrange the fillings evenly across the bottom third of the nori. With your thumbs, lift the edge of the nori that's closest to you. Using your fingers to keep the filling in place, roll the edge of the nori away from you so that it just slightly tucks under the filling. Continue to roll the nori, jelly-roll style, into a tight cylinder, making sure there are no air pockets. The seam should be on the bottom. Place a piece of plastic wrap over the roll. Place a bamboo mat over the plastic wrap, and shape into a squarish roll. Remove the mat and plastic wrap. Make sure that the ends are tucked in so the roll doesn't fall apart when you cut it. Using a sharp knife, cut crosswise into 8 equal pieces.

HORIZONTAL URAMAKI EXAMPLE: ## The "Original" California Roll

Makes 1 roll

You don't see the good ole California Roll around much anymore in these "creative sushi" days. How funny, since it's the dish that really started the whole craze in this country. I think our version, inside-out with the alfalfa sprouts on it, is awesome. We're talking crunchy cucumber, buttery smooth avocado, and sprouts. Now that's California ... and I love it.

- 6 tablespoons cooked blue crabmeat
- 2 tablespoons imitation crabmeat
- 2 tablespoons mayonnaise
- $^1/_2$ sheet, cut lengthwise, nori (dried seaweed)
- $^1/_2$ cup Sushi Rice (page 76)
- 1 teaspoon white sesame seeds, toasted (page 16)
- 2 ($^1/_4$ by 5-inch) sticks Japanese cucumber
- $^1/_4$ avocado, peeled, pitted, and sliced
- $^1/_2$ cup loosely packed alfalfa sprouts

In a small bowl, mix the blue crabmeat, imitation crabmeat, and mayonnaise. Keep chilled until ready to use.

To assemble the roll, place the nori, shiny-side down, on a cutting board with the long side closest to you. Spread the rice evenly on the nori. Sprinkle the rice with the sesame seeds. Flip the nori over, so the rice side is facing down and the nori side is facing up. Place the crab mixture, cucumber, and avocado evenly across the bottom third of the nori. Complete the roll, following the technique to make horizontal uramaki, but before wrapping the roll with plastic wrap, coat the outside of the roll with the alfalfa sprouts. Use plastic wrap and a bamboo mat to shape into a squarish roll. Remove the mat and plastic wrap and cut into 8 pieces. Serve with shoyu, wasabi, and gari.

Vertical Uramaki (Inside-out tatemaki)

On a clean, dry cutting board, place the nori, shiny-side down and with the short side closest to you. Spread the rice evenly to cover the entire nori. If the recipe call for sesame seeds, sprinkle over the rice. Flip the nori over so the rice side is facing down and the nori side is facing up. With the short side still closest to you, arrange the fillings evenly across the bottom third of the nori. With your thumbs, lift the edge of the nori that's closest to you. Using your fingers to keep the filling in place, roll the edge of the nori away from you so that it just slightly tucks under the filling. Continue to roll the nori, jelly-roll style, into a tight cylinder, making sure there are no air pockets. The seam should be on the bottom. Place a piece of plastic wrap over the roll. Place a bamboo mat over the plastic wrap, and shape into a squarish roll. Remove the mat and plastic wrap. Make sure that the ends are tucked in so the roll doesn't fall apart when you cut it. Using a sharp knife, cut crosswise into 8 equal pieces.

VERTICAL URAMAKI EXAMPLE: Sansei Special Roll

Makes 1 roll

Now this is a roll! I used to take two of these rolls and four beers into the movie theater instead of popcorn. Better than popcorn, even better than a girlfriend! You've got to remember to wear a black T-shirt though, not a white T-shirt like I used to. Otherwise, you come out with chili spots all over your shirt.

1/2 sheet, cut lengthwise, nori (dried seaweed)
1/2 cup Sushi Rice (page 76)
1 tablespoon furikake (rice seasoning)
1/4 cup Spicy Crab Mix (page 77)
1 (1/4 by 4-inch) stick Japanese cucumber
1 slice avocado
14 kaiware sprouts
2 tablespoons sweet Thai chili sauce

To assemble the roll, place the nori, shiny-side down, on a cutting board with the short side closest to you. Spread the rice evenly on the nori. Sprinkle the rice with the furikake. Flip the nori over, so the rice side is facing down and the nori side is facing up. Place the spicy crab mix, cucumber, avocado, and sprouts evenly across the bottom third of the nori. Complete the roll, following the technique to make vertical uramaki. Use plastic wrap and a bamboo mat to shape into a squarish roll. Remove the mat and plastic wrap and cut into 6 pieces. Arrange the pieces on a plate and drizzle on top with the sweet Thai chili sauce.

Sushi and Sashimi

Caterpillar Roll

What else would you name a sushi roll that looks like the body of a caterpillar in different hues of green and yellow? Looks good enough to eat.

$^1/_2$ sheet, cut lengthwise, nori (dried seaweed)

$^1/_2$ cup Sushi Rice (page 76)

1 teaspoon white sesame seeds, toasted (page 16)

2 (1-ounce) pieces prepared freshwater eel (unagi), heated (page 21)

2 ($^1/_4$ by 5-inch) sticks Japanese cucumber

$^1/_2$ avocado, thinly sliced crosswise

2 tablespoons smelt roe (masago)

$^1/_2$ cup mesclun (mixed salad greens)

2 tablespoons Unagi Sauce (page 89)

On a clean, dry cutting board, place the nori, shiny-side down and with the short side closest to you. Spread the rice evenly to cover the entire nori. Sprinkle the sesame seeds on top. Flip the nori over so the rice side is facing down and the nori side is facing up. With the short side still closest to you, evenly stack the unagi and cucumber across the bottom third of the nori. Complete the roll, following the technique to make vertical uramaki (page 40).

Layer the avocado to cover the length of the roll. Place a piece of plastic wrap over the roll, then place a bamboo mat over the plastic wrap and shape into a squarish roll. Remove the mat. With the plastic wrap still on and using a sharp knife, cut the roll into 8 equal pieces (leaving the plastic wrap on helps keep the avocado on top). Remove the plastic wrap. Arrange the pieces on a plate in the shape of a snake. Top each piece with ½ tablespoon masago. Serve with the mixed greens drizzled with the unagi sauce.

Gari Saba Roll with Citrus Wasabi Sauce

Makes 1 roll

When I was on a diet, one of my customers told me about this sauce because it has no sodium in it. I thought it was so weird, because who would think of combining lemon juice with wasabi? But because I was desperate for flavor, I tried it instead of the regular wasabi soy sauce. The sauce combined with mackerel was so phenomenal, it became a special roll for me. Try it, you'll like it.

CITRUS WASABI SAUCE

$1/2$ teaspoon wasabi paste

Juice of $1/2$ lemon

2 ounces marinated mackerel (saba) (page 18), coarsely chopped (about $1/4$ cup)

1 teaspoon thinly sliced green onion, green part only

1 tablespoon gari (pickled ginger), coarsely chopped

$1/2$ sheet, cut lengthwise, nori (dried seaweed)

1 cup Sushi Rice (page 76)

1 ($1/4$ by 4-inch) stick Japanese cucumber

1 piece pickled burdock (gobo)

$1/4$ cup kaiware sprouts

To prepare the sauce, in a small bowl, mix the wasabi and lemon juice. Set aside.

In another bowl, mix the mackerel, green onion, and gari together.

On a bamboo mat, place the nori, shiny-side down and with the short side closest to you. Spread the rice evenly on the nori, leaving a 1-inch border across the top. Spread the mackerel mixture evenly across the bottom third of the rice. Stack the cucumber, gobo, and sprouts on top of the mixture, positioning the leaf ends of the sprouts toward the outer edges of the roll. Use the bamboo mat to complete the roll, following the technique to make tatemaki (page 36). Using a sharp knife, cut crosswise into 6 equal pieces. Arrange on a plate and serve with the citrus wasabi sauce for dipping.

Grilled Veggie Roll

Makes 1 roll

Here's something for the vegetarian in the crowd. It's full of great flavors as well as having a great presentation.

2 shiitake mushroom caps, sliced

1 (4 by 1-inch) slice red bell pepper

1 (4 by 1-inch) slice yellow squash

2 tablespoons olive oil

Kosher salt and freshly ground black pepper

1/2 sheet, cut lengthwise, nori (dried seaweed)

1/2 cup Sushi Rice (page 76)

1 tablespoon furikake (rice seasoning)

2 slices avocado

Prepare a fire in a charcoal grill, or preheat a gas grill.

In a small bowl, toss the mushrooms, bell pepper, and squash in the olive oil. Season with salt and pepper. Place the vegetable mixture on the grill rack and grill, turning once, 2 minutes per side, or until lightly browned.

On a piece of plastic wrap, place the nori, shiny-side down and with the short side closest to you. Spread the rice evenly on the nori, leaving a ½-inch border across the top. Sprinkle the furikake on top of the rice. Flip the nori over, so the rice side is facing down and the nori side is facing up. Evenly stack the grilled vegetables and avocado across the bottom third of the nori. Complete the roll, following the technique to make vertical uramaki (page 40). Remove the plastic wrap. Using a sharp knife, cut crosswise into 4 or 6 equal pieces. Serve with shoyu, wasabi, and gari.

Kapalua Butterfry Roll

Makes 1 roll

Our first restaurant is located within Maui's beautiful Kapalua Resort. The resort's logo is a butterfly. Since we fry this roll, we adjusted the name (pronunciation idiosyncrasies have nothing to do with it). In this recipe, we like to use a member of the snapper family, but you can use any white fish. Salted salmon comes highly salted, so be sure to rinse the salmon off before using.

1 sheet nori (dried seaweed)

2 ounces snapper or other white fish, thinly sliced

2 ounces salted salmon, rinsed and thinly sliced

1 1/2 cups mesclun (mixed salad greens)

1/2 cup Crab Mix (page 77)

1 (1/4 by 5-inch) stick carrot

Sushi Rice (page 76) or cooked short-grain rice, to seal the roll

1/2 cup all-purpose flour

1 cup tempura batter

1 cup panko (Japanese breadcrumbs)

Cottonseed, peanut, or canola oil for deep-frying

1 tablespoon julienned red bell pepper, for garnish

1 tablespoon chopped green onion, green part only, for garnish

1/4 cup Ponzu Sauce (page 82)

On a clean, dry surface, place the nori, shiny-side down. Lay the snapper across the bottom third of the nori. Place the salmon in a layer above the snapper, across the middle third of the nori. Spread 1 cup of the greens evenly over the snapper and salmon. Place the crab mix and carrot across the bottom third. Spread the rice across the top 1/2 inch of the nori (this is to seal the roll). With your thumbs, lift the edge of the nori that's closest to you. Using your fingers to keep the filling in place, roll the edge of the nori away from you so that it just slightly tucks under the filling. Continue to roll the nori, jelly-roll style, into a tight cylinder, making sure the seam is on the bottom.

Evenly coat the sushi roll with the flour, then dip into the tempura batter to cover completely, then coat evenly with panko. In a heavy saucepan, pour in the oil to a depth of

(continued)

continued from page 49

continued from page 49

3 inches and heat to 375°. Add the sushi roll to the oil and fry, turning with tongs to cook evenly, for about 1 minute, until golden brown. Using a slotted spoon, transfer the roll to paper towels to drain. Let stand until slightly cooled. Using a sharp knife, cut crosswise into 6 pieces. Arrange the remaining ½ cup greens on a plate and lay the sushi pieces on top. Sprinkle the bell pepper and green onion on top. Serve with the ponzu sauce.

Pink Cadillac

Makes 1 roll

This is the first roll for which we decided to use a colorful soybean wrap instead of the traditional nori. If you can't find mamenori, go ahead and use the regular nori (but then it will be a Black Cadillac instead).

½ sheet pink mamenori (soybean wrapper), or ½ lengthwise sheet nori (dried seaweed)

⅔ cup Sushi Rice (page 76)

2 (1-ounce) pieces prepared freshwater eel (unagi), heated (page 21)

1 cooked shrimp (ebi)

2 slices Tamago (Egg Omelet) (page 80)

1 slice avocado

1 (¼ by 4-inch) stick Japanese cucumber

¼ cup kaiware sprouts

1 tablespoon Unagi Sauce (page 89)

On a bamboo mat, right along its edge, place the mamenori. Spread the rice evenly on the mamenori, leaving a ½-inch border across the top. Stack the unagi, ebi, tamago, avocado, and cucumber across the bottom third of the mamenori. Place the sprouts on top of the filling, positioning the leaf ends of the sprouts toward the outer edges of the roll. With your thumbs, lift the edge of the mat that's closest to you. Using your fingers to keep the filling in place, roll the edge of the nori away from you so that it just slightly tucks under the filling. Continue to roll the nori, jelly-roll style and not too tight, into a cylinder, removing the mat as you go. Using a sharp knife, cut crosswise into 6 pieces and arrange on a plate. Drizzle on top with the unagi sauce.

PMS Roll

This roll is named after a regular customer I served at a sushi bar in Wailea, Maui, and it stands for Patricia McCormick Special Roll. At my sushi bar, you can have it your way— we can combine anything according to your taste. Patricia would come in regularly, and after I got to know her, she asked me to make a special roll for her, since by then I knew her likes and dislikes. It was hot, summertime, and she wanted something refreshing and pretty. And it is pretty: If you look at the roll in cross-section, you should see an outer black ring, followed by a white ring, then a red ring, and all green in the middle.

$1/2$ sheet, cut lengthwise, nori (dried seaweed)

1 cup Sushi Rice (page 76)

2 ounces sashimi-grade tuna, sliced

2 shiso (perilla) leaves

2 green leaf lettuce leaves

1 tablespoon thinly sliced green onion, green part only

1 ($1/4$ by 4-inch) stick Japanese cucumber

$1/4$ cup kaiware sprouts

Slice of lemon, for garnish

$1/2$ cup Ponzu Sauce (page 82)

On a bamboo mat, right along its edge, place the nori, shiny-side down and with the long side closest to you. Spread the rice evenly on the nori, leaving a 1-inch border across the top. Place the tuna across the middle of the rice. On top of the tuna, center the shiso and lettuce. In the middle of the greens, crosswise, place the green onion, cucumber, and kaiware sprouts, positioning the leaf ends of the sprouts toward the outer edges of the roll. With your thumbs, lift the edge of the mat that's closest to you. Using your fingers to keep the filling in place, roll the edge of the nori away from you so that it just slightly tucks under the filling. Continue to roll the nori, jelly-roll style, into a tight cylinder, removing the mat as you go. The seam should be on the bottom. Using a sharp knife, cut crosswise into 6 equal pieces and arrange on a plate. Garnish with the lemon and serve with the ponzu sauce.

Rainbow Roll

Makes 1 roll

Hawai'i is the land of rainbows—so many rainbows of all different types. Our rainbow is made up of salmon, tuna, and avocado and represents the brilliant colors of Hawai'i. Oh, and it's also an homage to the former name of our University of Hawai'i sports teams (Go 'Bows!).

6 tablespoons cooked blue crabmeat

2 tablespoons imitation crabmeat

1 tablespoon mayonnaise

$^1/_2$ sheet, cut lengthwise, nori (dried seaweed)

1 $^1/_2$ cups Sushi Rice (page 76)

1 teaspoon white sesame seeds, toasted (page 16)

2 ($^1/_4$ by 4-inch) sticks Japanese cucumber

6 slices avocado

2 ounces sashimi-grade ahi, sliced into 2 (3 by 1 $^1/_2$ by 3/8-inch) pieces

2 ounces salted salmon, rinsed and sliced into 2 (3 by 1 $^1/_2$ by 3/8-inch) pieces

In a small bowl, mix together the blue crabmeat, imitation crabmeat, and mayonnaise. Keep chilled until ready to use.

On a clean, dry cutting board, place the nori, shiny-side down and with the long side closest to you. Spread the rice evenly to cover the entire nori. Sprinkle the sesame seeds on top. Flip the nori over so the rice side is facing down and the nori side is facing up. With the long side still closest to you, arrange the crab mixture, cucumber, and 4 slices of the avocado evenly across the bottom third of the nori. Complete the roll, following the technique to make horizontal uramaki (page 39). Alternate slices of ahi, avocado, salmon, and avocado, slightly overlapping, along the top of the roll. Place a piece of plastic wrap over the roll, then place a bamboo mat over the plastic wrap and shape into a squarish roll. Remove the mat. With a sharp knife, cut crosswise into 8 equal pieces, using the plastic wrap to hold the pieces together. Remove the plastic wrap. Arrange the pieces on a plate and serve with shoyu, wasabi, and gari.

Soba Roll

Makes 1 roll

In Hawai'i, most days are really hot, and a cold soba salad is the best thing for lunch. I was thinking, now what if we made a roll using these same ingredients. It would make it easier to eat and still be the best thing for lunch. What I found out in my first try was to make sure the soba noodles are dry.

TSUYU SAUCE

- 1/2 tablespoon shoyu (Japanese soy sauce)
- 2 tablespoons Dashi (Japanese Soup Stock) (page 81)
- 1/2 tablespoon mirin (sweet rice wine)
- 1/2 sheet, cut lengthwise, nori (dried seaweed)
- 2 ounces soba noodles, cooked, drained, and very dry (about 1 cup)

- 2 shiso (perilla) leaves
- 1 (1/4 by 4-inch) stick Japanese cucumber
- 3 strips prepared kampyo (seasoned gourd) (page 23)
- 1 slice Tamago (Egg Omelet) (page 80)
- 1 (1-ounce) piece prepared freshwater eel (unagi), heated (page 21)
- 1 teaspoon finely chopped green onion, green part only, for garnish

To make the sauce, in a saucepan, combine the shoyu, dashi, and mirin and bring to a boil. Remove from the heat and let stand until cool.

On a bamboo mat, right along its edge, place the nori, shiny-side down and with the long side closest to you. Spread the noodles across the bottom two-thirds of the nori. Arrange the shiso along the bottom third. Stack the cucumber, kampyo, tamago, and unagi on top of the shiso. With your thumbs, lift the edge of the mat that's closest to you. Using your fingers to keep the filling in place, roll the edge of the nori away from you so that it just slightly tucks under the filling. Continue to roll the nori, jelly-roll style, into a tight cylinder, removing the mat as you go. The seam should be on the bottom. Using a sharp knife, cut crosswise into 4 equal pieces. Top with the green onion. Serve with the tsuyu sauce and wasabi.

Spicy Japanese BLT Roll

Makes 1 roll

Don't hold the mayo on this one! With a little bit of sambal, upcountry Maui greens, and Hau'ula tomatoes, it truly is a Japanese-Hawai'i BLT. Salmon skin skin gets crispy and has a great crunchy sea flavor after toasting. Be sure to remove as much of the meat that remains on the skin as you can, or it will be harder to get it truly crispy.

2 ounces salmon skin

1/2 sheet, cut lengthwise, nori (dried seaweed)

2/3 cup Sushi Rice (page 76)

1 teaspoon Masago Aioli (page 76)

1/2 teaspoon sambal (Indonesian chili paste)

2 teaspoons diced vine-ripened tomato

1/2 cup mesclun (mixed salad greens)

Preheat the broiler. Lay the salmon skin on a broiler pan and broil the skin until toasted and crispy, 5 to 8 minutes. Cooking time will vary depending on the amount of meat left on the skin, as the fat from the salmon will increase broiling time, so monitor closely. Let cool slightly, then slice into thin strips.

On a bamboo mat, place the nori, shiny-side down and with the short side closest to you. Spread the rice evenly on the nori, leaving a 1/2-inch border across the top. Arrange the masago aioli, sambal, salmon skin, tomato, and greens across the bottom third of the rice. Complete the roll, following the technique to make tatemaki (page 36). Using a sharp knife, cut crosswise into 6 equal pieces. Serve.

69 Roll

Makes 1 roll

One good thing on top of another: succulent, roasted unagi on top of a California roll. What makes ours different—and better!—is our special unagi glaze.

¹/₂ sheet, cut lengthwise, nori (dried seaweed)

¹/₂ cup Sushi Rice (page 76)

1 teaspoon white sesame seeds, toasted (page 16)

¹/₃ cup Crab Mix (page 77)

2 (¹/₄ by 4-inch) sticks Japanese cucumber

2 slices avocado

3 (1-ounce) pieces prepared freshwater eel (unagi), heated (page 21)

¹/₄ cup Unagi Sauce (page 89)

4 tablespoons smelt role (masago), for garnish

On a clean, dry cutting board, place the nori, shiny-side down and with the long side closest to you. Spread the rice evenly to cover the entire nori. Sprinkle the sesame seeds on top. Flip the nori over so the rice side is facing down and the nori side is facing up. With the long side still closest to you, arrange the crab mix, cucumber, and avocado on the bottom third of the nori. Complete the roll, following the technique to make horizontal uramaki (page 39). Lay the unagi lengthwise along the top of the roll. Place a piece of plastic wrap over the roll. Place a bamboo mat over the plastic wrap and shape into a squarish roll. Remove the mat. Using a sharp knife, cut crosswise into 8 equal pieces. Remove the plastic wrap. Spoon the unagi sauce on top of the unagi. Top each slice with ¹/₂ tablespoon of masago.

Takah Sushi Special Roll

Makes 1 roll

This roll is a modification of the original from Aspen, Colorado. We added shrimp to it and made it our own . . . with Casey's blessing.

- 1 sheet nori (dried seaweed)
- 1 cup Sushi Rice (page 76)
- 2 tablespoons Crab Mix (page 77)
- 2 (1/4 by 4-inch) sticks Japanese cucumber
- 2 slices avocado
- 2 ounces sashimi-grade tuna, sliced into 2 (3 by 1 1/2 by 3/8-inch) pieces
- 1 cooked shrimp (ebi)
- 1/4 cup smelt roe (masago), for garnish

On a clean, dry cutting board, place the nori, shiny-side down and with the short side closest to you. Spread the rice evenly to cover the entire nori. Flip the nori over so the rice side is facing down and the nori side is facing up. With the short side still closest to you, arrange the crab mix, cucumber, avocado, tuna, and ebi on the bottom third of the nori. With your thumbs, lift the edge of the nori that's closest to you. Using your fingers to keep the filling in place, roll the edge of the nori away from you so that it just slightly tucks under the filling. Continue to roll the nori, jelly-roll style, into a tight cylinder, making sure there are no air pockets. The seam should be on the bottom. Make sure that the ends are tucked in so the roll doesn't fall apart when you cut it. Coat the sushi with the masago, either by laying the masago on a plate and rolling the sushi in it or by sprinkling the masago over the sushi with a spoon. Place a piece of plastic wrap over the roll. Place a bamboo mat over the plastic wrap, and shape the sushi into a three-sided roll. Remove the mat and plastic wrap. Using a sharp knife, cut crosswise into 8 equal pieces. Serve with shoyu, wasabi, and gari.

Yellow Submarine

Makes 1 roll

When we decided to create a roll with bright yellow mamenori instead of the traditional nori, guess what happened? Lo and behold, we all started singin' the Beatles tune!

SUSHI SHRIMP

8 extra-large shrimp, deveined, with shell and tail attached

1 gallon ice water

$1/4$ cup plus 2 tablespoons kosher salt

2 cups Shrimp Marinade (page 97)

1 sheet yellow mamenori (soybean wrapper) or nori (dried seaweed)

1 cup Sushi Rice (page 76)

2 strips prepared kampyo (seasoned gourd) (page 23)

1 teaspoon chopped gari (pickled ginger)

2 ($1/4$ by 4-inch) sticks Japanese cucumber

2 teaspoons smelt roe (masago)

To prepare the shrimp, skewer the shrimp through the vein line so they are straight, using 1 skewer per shrimp. In a large pot, add $1/4$ cup of the salt to 1 gallon of water and bring to a boil. Boil the shrimp for $1\frac{1}{2}$ to 2 minutes, until the shrimp are just cooked through and opaque. Remove the shrimp and place immediately in the ice water until cool. Drain.

Remove the skewers and peel the shrimp. To butterfly the shrimp, slice lengthwise from the underside without cutting all the way through so the shrimp can lay flat. Sprinkle with the remaining 2 tablespoons of salt and let stand for 10 minutes, then rinse well and drain. Transfer the shrimp to a shallow dish. Pour the marinade over the shrimp, turning to coat evenly. Let stand for 10 minutes. Remove the shrimp from the marinade and drain. Set aside. This recipe calls for 2 shrimp, so either use the remaining shrimp to make additional rolls, or store, covered, in the refrigerator for up to 3 days.

On a bamboo mat, right along its edge, place the mamenori. Spread the rice evenly on the mamenori, leaving a $1/2$-inch border across the top. Stack 2 shrimp, the kampyo, gari, cucumber, and masago across the bottom third of the rice. With your thumbs, lift the edge of the mat that's closest to you. Using your fingers to keep the filling in place, roll the edge of the nori away from you so that it just slightly tucks under the filling. Continue to roll the nori, jelly-roll style, into a tight cylinder, removing the mat as you go. The seam should be on the bottom. Using a sharp knife, cut crosswise into 6 equal pieces and arrange on a plate. Serve with shoyu, wasabi, and gari.

Tempura Shrimp Hand Roll

Makes 4 hand rolls

We made this for "A Taste of Lahaina" several years ago . . . and had a line at our booth a mile long. The very first sensation you get is that hot and crispy tempura shrimp sticking out of the roll. So from the first bite, it's just fantastic. With every bite from then on, you get the great tastes of all the other ingredients. We eventually ran out at the culinary festival at which we introduced this dish, but I really believe it was the hit of that event. It's still one of our best sellers.

4 large shrimp, peeled and deveined

Cottonseed, peanut, or canola oil for deep-frying

1/2 cup all-purpose flour

1 cup tempura batter

2 sheets nori (dried seaweed), cut in half lengthwise

1/2 cup Sushi Rice (page 76)

1 tablespoon Masago Aioli (page 76)

4 (3-inch) pieces green onion, green part only

4 (1/4 by 3-inch) sticks Japanese cucumber

3/4 cup Unagi Sauce (page 89)

1/2 teaspoon white sesame seeds

Pull each shrimp by its head and tail section. Then lay each one down and lightly press to straighten and lengthen it. (This will prevent curling when cooking.) In a heavy saucepan, pour in the oil to a depth of 3 inches and heat to 350°. Evenly coat the shrimp with the flour, shaking off the excess. Dip the shrimp into the tempura batter. Add the shrimp to the

(continued)

continued from page 59

oil and fry, turning with tongs to cook evenly, about 4 minutes, until golden brown. Using a slotted spoon, transfer to paper towels to drain.

Place 1 half sheet of nori shiny-side down diagonally in the palm of your hand. With your other hand, spread the rice evenly over the quarter of the nori closest to your thumb. Spread 1 teaspoon masago aioli on the rice and top with 1 piece green onion and 1 stick cucumber. Dip 1 shrimp in the unagi sauce and stack on top of the vegetables. Sprinkle with the sesame seeds. Using your free hand, fold the opposite corner of the nori over the filling and shape into a cone. Repeat to make 4 hand rolls.

Étouffée Roll of Shrimp and Crab

Makes 1 roll

In New Orleans, one of the dishes I enjoyed the most was a shrimp étouffée. When I got home, I wanted to create a roll with the same luscious étouffée sauce. We added shrimp and crab, and it came out great. You'll want a spoon to get every bit of the sauce.

ÉTOUFFÉE SAUCE

2 teaspoons kosher salt

2 teaspoons cayenne pepper

1 teaspoon freshly ground white pepper

1 teaspoon freshly ground black pepper

1 teaspoon dried sweet basil leaves

1/2 teaspoon dried thyme leaves

7 tablespoons vegetable oil

3/4 cup all-purpose flour

1/4 cup chopped onion

1/4 cup chopped celery

1/4 cup cored, seeded, and chopped green bell pepper

3 cups seafood or chicken stock

1 cup unsalted butter, at room temperature

1/4 cup cooked rock shrimp, coarsely chopped

1/4 cup cooked crabmeat, coarsely chopped

2 tablespoons mayonnaise

1/2 teaspoon Cajun blackening seasoning

1/2 sheet, cut lengthwise, nori (dried seaweed)

1/2 cup Sushi Rice (page 76)

2 asparagus spears, blanched

1/4 cup flying fish roe (tobiko)

1 tablespoon finely chopped green onion, green part only, for garnish

To make the sauce, in a small bowl, combine the salt, cayenne, white pepper, black pepper, basil, and thyme. Set aside. In a saucepan, heat the oil over high heat until it begins to shimmer. Reduce the heat to medium and gradually stir in the flour until smooth. Continue cooking, stirring constantly, until the mixture (called a roux) is a dark reddish brown,

(continued)

continued from page 61

5 to 7 minutes. Remove from the heat and immediately stir in the onion, celery, bell pepper, and the spice mixture, stirring until cool. In another saucepan, add the stock and bring to a boil. Gradually add the vegetable mixture and stir to combine. Whisk in the butter; the sauce will thicken as the butter is incorporated. Keep warm.

Squeeze all the liquid out of the shrimp and crab. Transfer to a small bowl and add the mayonnaise and blackening seasoning. Set aside.

On a clean, dry cutting board, place the nori, shiny-side down and with the long side closest to you. Spread the rice evenly on the nori, leaving a ½-inch border across the top. Flip the nori over so the rice side is facing down and the nori side is facing up. With the long side still closest to you, arrange the shrimp-crab mixture and the asparagus across the bottom one-third of the roll. Complete the roll, following the technique to make horizontal uramaki (page 39). Coat the sushi with the tobiko, either by laying the tobiko on a plate and rolling the sushi in it or by sprinkling the tobiko over the sushi with a spoon. Place a piece of plastic wrap over the roll. Place a bamboo mat over the plastic wrap and shape into a squarish roll. Remove the mat and plastic wrap. Using a sharp knife, cut crosswise into 8 equal pieces.

To serve, arrange the pieces on a plate in a fan shape. Pour about ½ cup of the sauce over the bottom half of the "fan" and on the plate in front of the roll. (Serve any remaining sauce on the side.) Sprinkle the green onion over all.

Teriyaki Snapper Nigiri

Serves 4 as an appetizer

Like our Foie Gras Nigiri (page 66), another good way to upgrade the simple nigiri preparation is with the Honey-Sesame Butter Sauce we use in this dish. We marinate the snapper, sear it, put in on nigiri with some vegetables, and finish it with a rich sauce.

$^1/_2$ cup rice vinegar

$^1/_2$ cup sugar

$^1/_4$ cup julienned carrot

1 cup Teriyaki Sauce (page 90)

8 ounces sashimi-grade snapper, cut into 8 slices

1 $^1/_2$ cups Sushi Rice (page 76)

1 cup kaiware sprouts

8 (4 by $^1/_2$-inch) strips nori (dried seaweed)

$^1/_4$ cup Honey-Sesame Butter Sauce (page 84)

In a small bowl, combine the vinegar and sugar and mix well. Add the carrot to the mixture and marinate for 5 minutes. Drain and set aside.

Pour the teriyaki sauce in a bowl. Add the snapper and marinate for 5 minutes. In a nonstick skillet over high heat, add the snapper and sear lightly for 30 seconds per side, until rare.

Divide the rice into 8 portions and, using your hands or a nigiri sushi mold, form into 2 by $^1/_2$-inch rectangles. Top each with 1 piece of snapper and one-eighth of the carrot and sprouts. Wrap each nigiri crosswise with 1 nori strip. Place 2 nigiri each on 4 small plates and drizzle 1 tablespoon of the warmed sauce over each pair.

Unagi and Avocado Nigiri with Raspberry Coulis

Serves 4 as an appetizer

This is a good one. We went up to Berkeley, California, and tasted something similar at a sushi bar there. They served fruit sauces with their sushi and it made quite an impression on me. Years later, we created this dish at a benefit for a fellow chef.

RASPBERRY COULIS

> 2 cups fresh raspberries
>
> 1 1/2 cups sugar
>
> 1 1/2 cups Sushi Rice (page 76)
>
> 8 slices avocado
>
> 8 (1-ounce) pieces prepared freshwater eel (unagi), heated (page 21)
>
> 8 (5 by 1/4-inch) strips nori (dried seaweed)

To prepare the coulis, in a small saucepan, combine the raspberries and sugar. Cook over medium heat for 20 minutes, until the raspberries have broken down and incorporated into the sauce. Transfer the mixture to a food processor and purée until smooth, about 2 minutes. Strain the mixture through a fine-mesh sieve to remove the seeds. Chill for at least 1 hour before using.

To prepare the nigiri, divide the rice into 8 portions and, using your hands or a nigiri sushi mold, form into 2 by 1/2-inch rectangles. Top each with 1 avocado slice and 1 piece of unagi. Wrap each nigiri crosswise with 1 nori strip. To serve, place 2 nigiri each on 4 small plates and drizzle each plate with the coulis.

Sweet Miso Scallop Nigiri with Yuzu Butter Sauce and Unagi Sauce

Serves 4 as an appetizer

This is another upscale nigiri sushi. For this one, we use jumbo scallops marinated with our own Asian miso barbecue sauce.

8 sea scallops

1 cup Miso Marinade (page 96)

1 teaspoon canola oil

1 1/2 cups Sushi Rice (page 76)

1/2 cup kaiware sprouts

8 (5 by 1-inch) strips nori (dried seaweed)

1 cup Yuzu Butter Sauce (page 87)

1 tablespoon Unagi Sauce (page 89)

1 tablespoon flying fish roe (tobiko), for garnish

1 tablespoon finely chopped gari (pickled ginger), for garnish

Butterfly each scallop by laying it flat-side down, slicing three-quarters of the way through, and opening up flat. Transfer to a shallow dish and pour the marinade over the scallops. Cover and refrigerate for at least 24 hours.

In a nonstick saute pan, heat the oil over high heat. Add the scallops, searing on both sides until golden brown, 2 to 3 minutes. Set aside and let cool slightly, about 2 minutes.

Divide the rice into 8 portions and, using your hands or a nigiri sushi mold, form into 2 by 1/2-inch rectangles. Top each with 1 scallop and a few sprouts. Wrap each nigiri crosswise with 1 nori strip. To serve, drizzle each of 4 plates with 1/4 cup of the yuzu butter sauce and dot with the unagi sauce. Place 2 nigiri on each plate and top each with a little of the tobiko and gari.

Foie Gras Nigiri

Serves 4 as an appetizer

We wanted to do something interesting—and Japanese—with one of my favorite foods of all time: foie gras. We were looking for simplicity combined with decadence. We definitely did not want to mask the foie gras. Nigiri is the perfect vehicle: The unagi glaze, fresh mango, and caramelized Maui onion provide exactly the right balance to this dish. Foie gras comes in lobes, with two distinct lobes on the liver and a vein that runs through it to connect the organ. To devein, separate the lobes and use a paper towel to pull the vein out of the liver. Foie gras is best kept very cold, as it will be firm and easier to work with. To slice, lay it flat and cut across the lobes; use immediately.

2 tablespoons cottonseed, peanut, or canola oil

1/4 cup julienned Maui onion or other sweet onion

1/2 cup Unagi Sauce (page 89)

1 1/2 cups Sushi Rice (page 76)

8 ounces grade A foie gras, deveined and sliced into 8 pieces

8 (4 by 1-inch) strips nori (dried seaweed)

1/2 cup peeled and diced fresh mango

2 tablespoons chopped fresh chives, for garnish

2 tablespoons smelt roe (masago), for garnish

In a sauté pan, heat the oil over medium heat. Decrease the heat to medium-low, add the onion, and cook, stirring occasionally, until caramelized (but not charred), 15 to 20 minutes. Stir in 1 tablespoon of the unagi sauce and set aside.

Divide the rice into 8 portions and, using your hands or a nigiri sushi mold, form into 2 by 1/2-inch rectangles. Set aside.

In a nonstick skillet over medium-high heat, sear the foie gras for 2 minutes per side until each side is caramelized and slightly firm to the touch.

Top each nigiri with 1 piece of foie gras. Holding the foie gras in place, wrap each nigiri crosswise with 1 nori strip. To serve, place 2 nigiri each in the center of 4 small plates and drizzle the remaining unagi sauce over each. Divide the mango and caramelized onion and spoon on either side of the nigiri. Top with the chives and masago.

Fresh Hawaiian Ahi Carpaccio

Serves 4 as an appetizer

I love carpaccio—traditionally, it's raw, very thinly sliced and well-seasoned beef served with olive oil and capers. But Sansei is the "home of the other red meat" (ahi), so we make our carpaccio with ahi. To me, it's an even better "meat" to use for this dish—it's more fragrant and has just as much protein as beef. We add a little Thai twist to make it truly memorable.

THAI SAUCE

1 tablespoon freshly squeezed lime juice

1 teaspoon fish sauce (patis)

Dash of sambal (Indonesian chili paste)

$^1/_4$ teaspoon minced garlic

1 tablespoon sugar

12 ounces sashimi-grade ahi, thinly sliced

1 teaspoon lime zest

2 tablespoons shredded carrot

2 tablespoons coarsely chopped peanuts

$^1/_4$ cup fresh cilantro leaves

To prepare the Thai sauce, in a small bowl, combine the lime juice, fish sauce, sambal, garlic, and sugar. Stir until the sugar is dissolved and the mixture is well combined. Chill before serving.

Place a sheet of plastic wrap over the ahi and, using a meat pounder, pound the ahi flat. To serve, divide the ahi among 4 plates and place the ahi in the center of each plate. Drizzle the Thai sauce over the ahi. Sprinkle the lime zest, carrot, peanuts, and cilantro over each plate.

Chinese-Style Snapper Sashimi

Serves 4 as an appetizer

I think of this as an upscale local dish, which, I guess, is sort of like an uptown girl with a downtown guy. This preparation is most commonly used for a whole fish, and at the restaurant we would fillet the fish for you. Here, we've simplified the recipe so you don't have to deal with a whole fish, but it's just as delicious.

12 ounces sashimi-grade snapper, thinly sliced

1/4 teaspoon shichimi (seven-spice pepper)

2 tablespoons peeled and minced fresh ginger

2 tablespoons peanut oil

2 tablespoons sesame oil

1/4 cup chopped cilantro, plus 4 sprigs for garnish

2 tablespoons finely chopped green onion, green part only

4 tablespoons shoyu (Japanese soy sauce)

Arrange the snapper on 4 plates. Sprinkle with shichimi and top each slice with a small amount of the ginger.

Just before serving, in a small skillet, heat the peanut and sesame oil over high heat until it starts to smoke. Remove from the heat. Sprinkle the chopped cilantro and green onion over the snapper. Ladle 1 tablespoon of the hot oil mixture over each, followed by 1 tablespoon of the shoyu. Garnish each plate with a cilantro sprig. Serve immediately.

The Kenny G

Serves 4 as an appetizer

When I was working in Aspen, Kenny G, the well-known clarinetist, sat in front of my station at the sushi bar two of the three nights he was in town. I wanted to make his favorite sushi for him and what he wanted was the halibut sashimi . . . with fresh garlic. Garlic and sushi bars *do not* mix. Garlic permeates everything you use—hands, knives, cutting boards. The head sushi chef was looking at me with Samurai swords in his eyes: "Don't even think about doing that," I know he was thinking. So, I did it anyway. It was Kenny G! After the garlic, I poured ponzu and masago over the sashimi and voila! He and everyone else at the bar that night loved it. From then on, I was in the back before each shift . . . chopping garlic! Here's Sansei's version, using fresh snapper instead of halibut.

2 tablespoons grated daikon radish	1 teaspoon minced garlic
Pinch of cayenne pepper	1/4 cup smelt roe (masago)
10 ounces sashimi-grade snapper, cut into 32 thin slices	2/3 cup Ponzu Sauce (page 82)
4 shiso (perilla) leaves, plus 8 leaves cut into chiffonade	

In a small bowl, prepare momiji oroshi by mixing the daikon and cayenne pepper (more cayenne can be added if desired). Set aside.

Lay 5 snapper slices in a semicircle on the top half of each of 4 plates. Place 1 shiso leaf at the bottom of each semicircle. On a flat surface, arrange 3 slices of snapper end-to-end lengthwise, overlapping slightly. Roll, then turn upright, opening it slightly so the configuration looks like a flower. Repeat three times. Place a "flower" on top of the shiso leaf on each plate.

On the snapper semicircle, place a tiny bit of garlic in the middle of each slice. On top of the garlic, place a little of the momiji oroshi. On top of that, place a little of the masago. Sprinkle the shiso chiffonade over each plate. Spoon the ponzu sauce around the rim of each plate to form a pool. Serve.

Ahi Poke

From professional chefs to home cooks to a favorite auntie or uncle, everyone in Hawai'i has his or her own version of ahi poke. Here is ours, made with some of my favorite things: a little spicy heat, a little sesame oil, ginger, and shoyu—for the oriental in me (when I first said this, my wife looked at me and said, "You're *all* oriental").

POKE SAUCE

- 1/2 cup shoyu (Japanese soy sauce)
- 1/4 cup Asian (toasted) sesame oil
- 2 tablespoons sambal (Indonesian chili paste)
- 2 tablespoons peeled and minced fresh ginger
- 1 teaspoon sea salt

- 8 ounces sashimi-grade ahi, finely diced
- 1/4 cup finely diced Japanese cucumber

- 1/4 cup finely sliced Maui onion or other sweet onion
- 2 tablespoons dried wakame (seaweed), rehydrated in warm water
- 2 tablespoons finely chopped green onion, green part only
- 1/2 cup kaiware sprouts
- 2 tablespoons smelt roe (masago)
- 1 tablespoon white sesame seeds, for garnish

To prepare the poke sauce, in a bowl, combine the shoyu, sesame oil, sambal, ginger, and salt until well blended. Chill before serving. The sauce can be prepared 1 day in advance, then covered and stored in the refrigerator until ready to use.

To prepare the poke, in another bowl, combine the ahi, cucumber, onion, wakame, green onion, sprouts, and masago. Add the sauce and toss gently to combine; do not overmix and use only enough of the sauce to coat. Divide the ahi mixture evenly among 4 plates and place the mixture in the center of each plate. Sprinkle a little of the sesame seeds over each plate. Serve immediately.

Shikomi and Sauces

Cooked Rice

Makes 8 cups

Rice is the single most important ingredient in sushi. It takes time to perfect the cleaning and cooking techniques as well as your own "eye." Rice is harvested only once a year, so it follows that the rice gets drier as the supply from any single harvest year begins to run out. The drier the rice, the more water it needs to cook properly. By the same token, when newly harvested rice comes onto the market, it needs less water. If you don't know the age of your rice—and you probably won't—it's going to take practice, practice, practice. After you make the rice, taste it: If it's too hard, you'll need to add more water next time; if it's too mushy, you'll need to use less water. As I said, practice makes perfect, and rice has to be perfect to make sushi. So, if you're making sushi, either use the imperfect rice for some-thing else (fried rice is good), or I'm afraid you'll have to throw it away.

5 cups short-grain white rice

Fill a large bowl two-thirds full with cold water. Put the rice into a colander that fits inside the bowl. Submerge the colander in the bowl of water. Gently rub the rice in your hands to remove the talc. Drain the cloudy water. Repeat this process until the water is clear.

Drain the rice and transfer it to a rice cooker. Add 5 cups water. Cook the rice in the rice cooker, 15 to 25 minutes. Let rest for 15 minutes before serving or using to make Sushi Rice (page 76). Store leftover rice in a covered container in the refrigerator.

Shari Zu (Sushi-Su)

Makes 1 1/2 cups

Another sushi bar standard, and everyone has their own version. This is ours. The thing you have to remember when adding this to rice is that the resulting sushi rice is not the star attraction when you eat it. For the rice to be perfect, the shari zu should be like a butler, like a good supporting actor: the star attraction is everything else besides the rice. It's definitely a balancing act. Besides adding flavor, shari zu is also a method of preserving the sushi rice.

1 cup rice vinegar

2/3 cup sugar

2 tablespoons kosher salt

1 (1-inch-square) piece konbu (kelp)

In a saucepan, add the vinegar and bring to a boil over high heat. Add the sugar and salt and stir to combine. Decrease the heat to medium and cook until the sugar and salt have dissolved, about 5 minutes. Remove from the heat and add the konbu. Allow to cool before using. This amount will season 16 cups of cooked rice. Store in an airtight container in the refrigerator for up to 1 month.

Sushi Rice

Makes 2 cups

There's no sushi without sushi rice. To get it right, you must use a wooden spoon and you must mix very gently.

>   2 cups hot cooked rice (page 74)
>
>   6 tablespoons Shari Zu (page 75)

After cooking the rice, transfer to a rice tub or wooden bowl. Pour the shari zu over all the rice. Using a rice paddle or wooden spoon, mix (or "cut") the rice gently with a slicing motion. Make sure all the grains are seasoned with the shari zu, but be very careful not to overmix, or the rice will get mushy. This whole process must be done quickly. Spread the rice evenly in the tub. After 10 minutes, turn the rice over and let it rest until cool. Transfer the rice to an insulated container to keep it from drying out.

Masago Aioli

Makes 1 cup

This is the workhorse sauce of all modern sushi bars. It gives everything a richer and creamier taste and enhances the flavors in many dishes. The garlic makes ours different.

>   1 cup mayonnaise
>
>   3 tablespoons smelt roe (masago)
>
>   1 teaspoon finely chopped garlic

In a small bowl, combine all the ingredients and mix well. Store in an airtight container in the refrigerator for up to 1 month.

Crab Mix

Makes 1 cup

Crab mix is as essential as it is versatile. Happily, it couldn't be easier to make. You'll find it used in several sushi recipes in this book.

1 cup cooked crabmeat (any kind)

2 tablespoons mayonnaise

Squeeze all the liquid from the crab. In a bowl, combine the crab and mayonnaise. Mix well. Store in an airtight container in the refrigerator for up to 3 days.

Spicy Crab Mix

Makes about 1 cup

This mix is the basis for our Sansei Special Roll (page 41). We also use it in our Rock Shrimp and Spicy Crab Lumpia recipe (page 116). It can be used in salads, as a stuffing for shellfish, or let your imagination run wild.

6 tablespoons cooked blue crabmeat

2 tablespoons imitation crabmeat

2 tablespoons mayonnaise

2 tablespoons smelt roe (masago)

$1/2$ teaspoon sambal (Indonesian chili paste)

2 tablespoons finely chopped fresh cilantro

Squeeze all the liquid from the crab. In a bowl, combine all the ingredients and mix well. Store in an airtight container in the refrigerator for up to 3 days.

Spicy Tuna Mix

Makes 1 cup

Every sushi bar stocks some kind of tuna mix, another versatile filling. Ours has a nice kick.

3 ounces sashimi-grade tuna, chopped

2 tablespoons Masago Aioli (page 76)

1 teaspoon smelt roe (masago)

1/8 teaspoon sambal (Indonesian chili paste)

1 teaspoon finely chopped green onion, green part only

1/8 teaspoon Asian (toasted) sesame oil

Pinch of cayenne pepper, or more to taste

In a bowl, combine all the ingredients and mix well. Cover and refrigerate until ready to use. May be made 1 day in advance.

Marinated Salmon Roe

Makes about 2 cups

Most sushi bars will just get ikura from a purveyor and serve it as it comes. All it is, is salty. If you wash and marinate the roe, you end up with a better flavor.

2 cups sake

2 tablespoons mirin (sweet rice wine)

1/4 cup shoyu (Japanese soy sauce)

1 pound salmon roe (ikura)

In a saucepan, heat the sake over medium-high heat until the alcohol is cooked off, about 5 minutes. Remove from the heat. Add the mirin and shoyu and stir to combine. Chill until completely cool.

Place the salmon roe in a colander or strainer, immerse it in cold water and gently shake it to wash off some of the salt. Pick out all bits that are on the roe sac membranes. Repeat this process three times, changing the water each time. Gently drain off the excess water and transfer the roe to the marinade. Let stand for 20 minutes or until all the eggs are plump. Transfer the plumped roe back to the colander to strain. Serve immediately. Store the salmon roe in an airtight container in the refrigerator for no more than 4 days.

Tamago (Egg Omelet)

This slightly sweet, layered Japanese omelet is such a basic food item here in Hawai'i, it's available at Seven-Eleven stores! It is used both as a sushi topping (always plain) and as part of a plate lunch (once you get the recipe and technique down, you can experiment by adding dried shrimp, bacon, or anything else you would like to try). When cooking, use a nonflavored oil so as not to impart additional flavorings, and be careful not to brown the omelet—it should have a nice pale yellow color and a firm texture. Rectangular pans specially designed just to make these omelets can be purchased at Japanese markets; a nonstick skillet will also work, although you won't get the nice square edges.

> 1 tablespoon sugar
>
> Pinch of kosher salt
>
> 1/2 teaspoon shoyu (Japanese soy sauce)
>
> 1 tablespoon mirin (sweet rice wine)
>
> 1 tablespoon half-and-half
>
> 10 eggs
>
> 1 teaspoon vegetable oil plus additional oil to repeat cooking

In a saucepan, combine 2 cups water with the sugar, salt, shoyu, mirin, and half-and-half and heat over medium-high heat to bring the mixture to a boil. Reduce the heat to a simmer and cook for 5 minutes, to cook off the alcohol and blend the flavors. Let cool.

In a bowl, whip the eggs to a fluffy consistency. Add the cooled mixture to it and stir to combine.

In a square omelet pan, heat 1 teaspoon of the oil over medium heat to just before it starts to smoke, about 2 minutes. Pour ½ cup of the egg mixture into the pan and roll the pan back and forth to form a thin sheet. Use a pair of chopsticks to break any bubbles that appear on the surface. When the omelet just begins to set, with the chopsticks pick up the end of the omelet closest to the handle and fold it to the other end. Leaving the omelet in the pan, repeat the process: add a little more oil, then add ½ cup of the egg mixture to coat the base of the pan, carefully lifting the cooked omelet to allow the mixture to run underneath. When the omelet just begins to set, fold it to the other end, wrapping it around the previously cooked omelet. Repeat until the egg mixture is used up and you have a rectangular omelet that is roughly 6 inches long by 3½ inches wide by 1½ inches thick. Let cool, then slice crosswise into 10 to 12 slices. The tamago can be made several hours in advance and stored in plastic wrap in the refrigerator until ready to use.

Dashi (Japanese Soup Stock)

Makes 2 cups

This is the foundation of the Japanese soup broth and is also a great base for sauces. It is slightly smoky and lends an added dimension and depth of flavor to the soup or sauce that you are creating.

- 1 (3-inch-square) piece konbu (kelp)
- ¹/4 cup katsuobushi (bonito flakes)

Rinse the konbu under running water to remove its residue. In a saucepan, combine the konbu, 2 cups water, and the katsuobushi over high heat and bring almost to a boil over high heat. Remove from the heat and strain the liquid through a sieve lined with cheesecloth. Let cool. Store in an airtight container in the refrigerator for up to 3 days.

Ponzu Sauce

Makes 6 cups

Every sushi bar has its own house ponzu sauce. The base of this sauce is similar to that used in other restaurants, but adding the fresh fruit right before serving sets it apart and gives it that extra "oomph." Up to 1 day before serving, add a squeeze of any citrus fruit per 2 cups of ponzu. Orange will make it sweeter; lemon or lime will make it more tart.

- $1/2$ cup sake
- $1/2$ cup mirin (sweet rice wine)
- 1 cup yuzu (Japanese citrus) juice
- 2 cups shoyu (Japanese soy sauce)
- 1 cup rice vinegar
- 1 (3-inch-square) piece konbu (kelp)

In a saucepan, cook the sake and mirin over high heat until the alcohol is cooked off, about 2 minutes. Add the remaining ingredients along with 1 cup water, stirring to combine well. Store in an airtight container in the refrigerator for up to 1 month.

Black Bean Paste

Makes 1 cup

Black bean sauce is essential to Pacific Rim cooking, and this is the base for any good black bean sauce. It works particularly well with fish and shellfish—we use it in our recipe for Steamed Moi (page 193). Salted black beans (do not confuse these with dry turtle beans) are fermented black soybeans and can be found in Asian markets.

- $1/2$ cup salted black beans
- 1 teaspoon peeled and sliced fresh ginger
- 1 teaspoon chopped garlic
- 1 teaspoon sambal (Indonesian chili paste)
- 1 teaspoon chopped green onion, green part only
- $1/2$ cup Asian (toasted) sesame oil

In a bowl, soak the beans in warm water for at least 20 minutes. Rinse to remove some of the salt cure.

In a food processor, combine the beans with the remaining ingredients. Pulse until thoroughly mixed and smooth in texture. Store in an airtight container in the refrigerator for up to 1 month.

Honey-Sesame Butter Sauce

Makes 1 cup

This is such a wonderful sauce: The richness of the butter and the natural sweetness of the honey balance out the earthy tones from the sesame oil. This sauce appears in three of our recipes in this cookbook, but it is so versatile that you can experiment with it and the amount can be increased without any problems.

- 1 cup sake
- 1 teaspoon peeled and minced fresh ginger
- 1 cup heavy cream
- 1 teaspoon Asian (toasted) sesame oil
- 2 tablespoons honey
- 1/4 cup unsalted butter
- Kosher salt and freshly ground black pepper

In a saucepan, cook the sake and ginger over medium-high heat until reduced by half, about 12 minutes. Add the cream, decrease the heat to medium, and reduce by half again, stirring occasionally, about 10 minutes. Decrease the heat to medium-low, add the oil and honey, and stir until combined. Add the butter and whisk until smooth. Season with salt and pepper. Keep warm until ready to use.

Ginger-Lime-Chili Butter Sauce

Makes 2 cups

A former chef created the basic recipe for this sauce for our Asian Rock Shrimp Cake (page 121). The very first night we were going to serve it (30 minutes before dinner service!), I tasted it and didn't think it was good enough—it needed a "wow" factor. So I added the sweet Thai chili sauce. The sauce—and the dish—has been a hit ever since. We also use it with our Restaurant Row Escargot (page 161).

1 tablespoon cottonseed, peanut, or canola oil

1 teaspoon minced shallot

¹/4 cup dry white wine

1 teaspoon peeled and coarsely chopped fresh ginger

Juice of 1 lime

6 tablespoons heavy cream

¹/2 cup unsalted butter

Kosher salt

¹/4 cup sweet Thai chili sauce

In a sauté pan, heat the oil over medium-high heat. Add the shallots and sauté until translucent, about 2 minutes. Add the wine, ginger, and lime juice and cook until reduced by half, about 12 minutes. Add the cream and cook to reduce by half again, about 10 minutes. Whisk in the butter and season with salt. Remove from the heat and strain through a fine-mesh sieve. Whisk in the sweet Thai chili sauce until well combined. Keep warm until ready to use. The sauce is at its optimum flavor and texture when used fresh, but if necessary, the sauce can be prepared ahead of time and stored in an airtight container in the refrigerator for up to 4 days. To reheat the sauce, transfer to a saucepan over medium heat and slowly bring back to temperature. The butter will separate. Remove the butter and slowly whisk it back into the warmed sauce to incorporate.

Soy-Wasabi Butter Sauce

Makes 1 cup

We created this sauce for our Panko-Crusted Ahi Sashimi (page 136). We started with just the soy and wasabi, but it was too sharp. The butter really smoothes it out. You can use it with any fish that you would use soy and wasabi with. It hits all four notes: sweet, sour, salty and bitter. It's one of our most perfect sauces.

1 tablespoon cottonseed, peanut, or canola oil

1 teaspoon minced shallot

1/2 cup dry white wine

1 tablespoon peeled and minced fresh ginger

1 teaspoon freshly squeezed lime juice

1/4 cup heavy cream

1/2 cup unsalted butter

3 tablespoons sweet Thai chili sauce

1 tablespoon wasabi paste

6 tablespoons shoyu (Japanese soy sauce)

In a saucepan, heat the oil over medium-high heat. Add the shallots and sauté until translucent, 1 to 2 minutes. Add the wine, ginger, and lime juice and cook until reduced by half, about 12 minutes. Add the cream and cook to reduce by one-third, about 10 minutes. Whisk in the butter until smooth. Remove from the heat and strain through a fine-mesh sieve. Stir in the chili sauce. In a small bowl, combine the wasabi and shoyu. Whisk the wasabi mixture into the butter sauce until smooth. Keep warm until ready to use.

Yuzu Butter Sauce

Makes 1 1/2 cups

The French have their beurre blanc. This is the Japanese version, which we use in a variety of dishes, such as Sweet Miso Scallop Nigiri (page 65), Scallop and Truffle Ravioli (page 115), and Rock Shrimp and Spicy Crab Lumpia (page 116).

1/4 cup yuzu (Japanese citrus) juice or fresh lemon juice

1/4 cup dry white wine

1/3 cup heavy cream

1 cup unsalted butter, at room temperature

Kosher salt and freshly ground black pepper

In a nonreactive saucepan, cook the yuzu juice, wine, and cream over medium-high heat until reduced by half, about 10 minutes. Transfer to a blender, add the butter, and blend until smooth and creamy, about 30 seconds. Season with salt and pepper. Keep warm until ready to use.

Su-Miso Sauce

Makes about 6 cups

This is a sushi bar standard; everyone has their own. Traditionally, this sauce was made for special occasions and was served with octopus or squid. Because it has such a wonderful flavor, we use it a lot—for example, in our Sansei Surf 'n' Turf (page 134), Miso Butterfish (page 139), and Miso Chicken (page 145). You can also try adding a little almond butter to it, which gives the sauce a nice nutty flavor.

2 cups mirin (sweet rice wine)

$1/2$ cup sake

2 cups sugar

1 $1/4$ cups white miso (soybean paste)

In a saucepan, cook the mirin and sake over high heat until the alcohol is cooked off, about 4 minutes. Decrease the heat to medium, add the sugar, and stir until dissolved. Whisk in the miso. Remove from the heat and let cool. Store in an airtight container in the refrigerator for up to 1 month.

Unagi Sauce

Makes about 4 cups

Like the fast-food joint in that old commercial, we have a "special sauce" too. This is it. Also known as Unagi Glaze, it's our secret weapon and one of our workhorse sauces. Amazingly, it works with almost everything. In the restaurant, we make it as it's traditionally made, with the heads and bones of anago (saltwater eel). This recipe tastes just like the real thing but is much easier to make. Hondashi is packaged dry "instant" dashi and can be found in Asian markets.

> 4 cups sake
>
> 1 cup mirin (sweet rice wine)
>
> 1 cup shoyu (Japanese soy sauce)
>
> 1 cup sugar
>
> 1 teaspoon hondashi (Japanese soup base)

In a large pot, add all the ingredients and cook over medium-high heat, slowly reducing to the consistency of a light syrup or a glaze, about 20 minutes. Watch it carefully: If it seems too thick, add a little water or more mirin to achieve the right consistency. Remove from the heat and let cool. The sauce will thicken as it cools. Store in an airtight container in the refrigerator for up to 1 month.

Teriyaki Sauce

Makes 6 cups

This is an absolutely essential pantry item for every Japanese kitchen or restaurant. Use it in the same way you'd use any barbecue sauce, when you want a Japanese touch.

2 1/2 cups shoyu (Japanese soy sauce)

1 3/4 cups mirin (sweet rice wine)

1 cup sugar

3 tablespoons peeled and minced fresh ginger

1 tablespoon minced garlic

2 tablespoons hondashi (Japanese soup base)

3 tablespoons cornstarch

In a large saucepan, combine the shoyu, mirin, sugar, ginger, garlic, hondashi, and 1 cup water and stir until the sugar is dissolved. Bring the mixture to a boil over medium-high heat. In a small bowl, combine the cornstarch and 3 tablespoons water, mixing until smooth. Add the cornstarch mixture to the shoyu mixture and simmer over low heat for 15 minutes, until thickened. Strain through a fine-mesh sieve and cool before using. Store in an airtight container in the refrigerator for up to 1 month.

Thai Vinaigrette

Makes about 1 cup

We use this on our award-winning Mango and Crab Salad Hand Roll (page 104). But you can use this with any summer roll or spring roll. It also makes a great salad dressing.

3 tablespoons sake

1/2 cup rice vinegar

1/2 cup sugar

1/2 tablespoon chopped garlic

3 tablespoons fish sauce (patis)

1 teaspoon sambal (Indonesian chili paste)

In a saucepan, cook the sake over high heat until the alcohol is cooked off, 1 to 2 minutes. Remove from the heat and let cool. Add the remaining ingredients and mix well. Chill before using. Store in an airtight container in the refrigerator for up to 1 month.

Umeboshi Vinaigrette

Makes 1 cup

Umeboshi is a pickled Japanese plum that is soaked in brine and red shiso (perilla) leaves. The salty and tart flavors of the umeboshi combine with the other ingredients to create an eye-appealing dressing with a refreshing, wonderful flavor that is most versatile in its uses. You can find both ume paste and ume sauce at Asian markets.

1 1/2 tablespoons ume (sour plum) paste

1 teaspoon ume sauce

3/4 cup rice vinegar

2 tablespoons sugar

1/2 tablespoon hondashi (Japanese soup base)

1/2 tablespoon minced shallot

1/2 teaspoon freshly ground white pepper

1/2 tablespoon shoyu (Japanese soy sauce)

1 teaspoon powdered mustard

1 teaspoon chopped garlic

3 tablespoons cottonseed, peanut, or canola oil

3 tablespoons soybean oil

In a blender or food processor, combine the ume paste and ume sauce and process until very smooth. Add the vinegar, sugar, hondashi, shallots, pepper, shoyu, mustard, and garlic and process until blended. Slowly add the oils and blend until emulsified. Store in an airtight container in the refrigerator for up to 2 weeks.

Truffle Butter

Makes 2 cups

Every household needs truffle butter. It makes any plain dish into a gourmet delight. Add it to a 99¢ package of ramen noodles and you have a $10 dish. White truffle oil is available in gourmet food stores. Yes, it's expensive and it's worth it. You'll find truffle peelings at gourmet food stores too. In fact, you can buy prepared truffle butter, but we prefer our house-made recipe.

1 teaspoon olive oil

$1/2$ tablespoon minced shallot

2 cups unsalted butter, at room temperature

1 tablespoon white truffle oil

1 tablespoon Madeira or dry white wine

$1/2$ teaspoon shoyu (Japanese soy sauce)

$1/2$ ounce truffle peelings

$1/4$ teaspoon chopped fresh chervil

$1/4$ teaspoon kosher salt

$1/4$ teaspoon freshly ground black pepper

In a small skillet, heat the oil over low heat. Add the shallots and cook until translucent, about 2 minutes, making sure they don't brown. In a large bowl, preferably of an electric mixer at medium speed, beat the butter, truffle oil, Madeira, shoyu, and cooked shallots, until smooth. By hand, fold in the truffle peelings and chervil and add the salt and pepper. Store in an airtight container in the refrigerator for up to 1 month, or freeze for up to 3 months.

Lobster Stock

Even though commercial lobster stock is available, there's nothing like the richness, flavor, and color of the homemade variety. Think of it as an affordable indulgence.

  3 pounds lobster heads

  1 large onion, diced

  1 cup diced carrot

  1 cup diced celery

  2 cloves garlic, halved

  $1/4$ cup tomato paste

  1 bay leaf

  2 teaspoons dried thyme

  1 tablespoon whole black peppercorns

Preheat the oven to 450°. Place the lobster in a roasting pan and roast for 10 minutes. Transfer the lobster to a large stockpot and add the remaining ingredients with enough water to cover. Simmer over medium heat for 1 hour. Strain. Return the pot to medium heat and simmer until reduced by half, about 20 minutes. Store refrigerated in an airtight container for up to 5 days or store in the freezer for up to 1 month.

Veal Demi-Glace

Makes about 4 cups

A good demi-glace is absolutely essential to a good pantry. There's none better than veal demi-glace. The finished glaze is rich and brown, with a beautiful shine and natural stickiness from the gelatin that has been released from the bones. The fragrance is one of clean and rich earthy beef tones. For additional richness, remove the marrow from the bones and use as a garnish, or just enjoy it anyway you like.

5 pounds veal bones	1 head garlic
1 pound onion, chopped	4 bay leaves
1 pound carrot, chopped	10 whole peppercorns
1 pound celery, chopped	1/4 cup tomato paste
1/2 pound leek, green part only, chopped	4 cups red wine

Preheat the oven to 375°. In a roasting pan, roast the veal bones for 45 minutes. Remove the pan from the oven and add the onion, carrot, celery, leek, garlic, bay leaves, peppercorns, and tomato paste. Return the pan to the oven and roast for 20 minutes.

Remove the pan from the oven and add the red wine, using a metal spatula to scrape up the browned bits from the bottom of the pan. Return the pan to the oven for about 10 minutes, until the liquid is reduced by a quarter.

Remove the pan from the oven and transfer the mixture to a 3-gallon stockpot. Add enough water to cover the bones by at least 2 inches. Gently simmer on low heat for at least 6 hours, until dark and glossy.

Remove from the heat and strain through a large sieve or colander set over a small stockpot. Heat the mixture over medium heat for about 1 hour, until it is reduced by two-thirds, leaving about 4 cups of rich demi-glace. Store in the freezer for up to 6 months or store, covered, in the refrigerator for 1 week. To reheat, thaw (if frozen), then transfer to a saucepan and slowly bring the sauce to a simmer over medium heat.

Unagi Demi-Glace

Makes about 6 cups

There's nothing like this demi-glace to go with any Japanese-style beef dish. The unagi adds just the right touch of sweet. It's a pretty nice match.

4 cups Veal Demi-Glace (page 95)	1 cup unsalted butter
1 1/2 cups Unagi Sauce (page 89)	Kosher salt and freshly ground black pepper

In a large saucepan, add the demi-glace, unagi sauce, and butter and bring to a boil. Remove from the heat. Check the seasoning and add salt and pepper, if needed. Store, covered, in the refrigerator for 1 week. To reheat, transfer to a saucepan and slowly bring to a simmer, stirring frequently, over medium heat.

Miso Marinade

Makes 5 cups

This is another Japanese barbecue sauce. It works as a basting sauce as well as a marinade. It works particularly well with chicken and oily fish, and it's best when ingredients are marinated in it for at least 24 hours (that time may, of course, be adjusted according to particular recipe instructions).

2 cups white miso (soybean paste)	1/2 cup mirin (sweet rice wine)
2 cups sugar	1/2 cup sake

In a bowl, combine the miso and sugar and mix well. Add the mirin and sake, mixing until smooth. Store in an airtight container in the refrigerator for up to 1 month.

Shrimp Marinade

In the olden days, when travelers in Japan took rice, fish, and shellfish on long journeys, they used a marinade just like this one. In addition to being a good preservative, it adds a lot of flavor.

> $1/3$ cup rice vinegar
>
> $1/3$ cup sugar
>
> Juice of 1 lemon

In a bowl, combine the vinegar, sugar, and 1 cup water. Add the lemon juice and mix well. Use immediately; do not store.

Edamame Mash

Makes 2 cups

A high-end, and very healthy, substitute for mashed potatoes. Frozen parboiled edamame may be used if fresh is not available.

> 2 cups fresh edamame (green soybeans)
>
> $1/4$ cup unsalted butter, at room temperature
>
> Kosher salt and freshly ground black pepper

In a pot, boil the edamame for about 30 minutes, until tender. Drain and let cool slightly, then remove the beans from their pods. In a food processor, blend the edamame until smooth. Add the butter and process until smooth. Season with salt and pepper.

Mashed Potatoes

Makes 4 cups

These potatoes will take you home. The creamy, buttery flavor and texture of the Yukon Gold potato are perfect for this classic preparation.

1 1/2 pounds Yukon Gold potatoes, peeled and diced into 1-inch cubes

1 cup heavy cream

2 tablespoons unsalted butter, at room temperature

Kosher salt and freshly ground black pepper

In a large saucepot, bring 1/2 gallon of salted water to a boil. Add the potatoes and cook for 20 minutes, until fork-tender. Drain. In a small saucepan, bring the cream just to a boil. Remove from the heat and set aside.

In a bowl, using a potato masher, mash the potatoes, cream, and butter until creamy. Season with salt and freshly ground black pepper.

Variation: To make Garlic Mashed Potatoes, add 3 cloves roasted garlic and mash with the other ingredients. Roasted garlic is available in supermarkets, or you can make it yourself by brushing a head of garlic with olive oil and baking, covered, for 20 minutes in a 400° oven. The garlic cloves will be soft and sweet.

Small Plates

Mango and Crab Salad Hand Roll with Thai Vinaigrette

Serves 4

Ah, the green (and pink, and yellow) mamenori. The mamenori, which comes in fluorescent colors and is much softer than regular nori, is really what makes the dish. (As mentioned before, mamenori is readily available in Hawaiʻi but is harder to find on the Mainland, where a few Asian markets carry it, or you can order it online.) This is one of our "A Taste of Lahaina" award winners—it won in the Best Salad category. The roll came first, then the sauce. It's one of our biggest hits to date, both in taste and presentation.

3 cups cooked blue crabmeat, chopped

1 cup imitation crabmeat, minced

1/4 cup mayonnaise

4 sheets mamenori (soybean wrapper), any color, or nori (dried seaweed)

2 teaspoons cooked short-grain white rice

8 cups loosely packed mesclun (mixed salad greens), extremely dry

2 cups peeled and diced fresh mango

1 cup dry-roasted peanuts

2 cups coarsely chopped fresh cilantro

1 medium Japanese cucumber, thinly sliced

1/2 cup Thai Vinaigrette (page 91)

3 tablespoons sweet Thai chili sauce

In a bowl, combine the blue crabmeat, imitation crabmeat, and mayonnaise. Mix well and set aside.

On a bamboo mat, lay 1 mamenori sheet. Spread 1/2 teaspoon of the rice in a very thin line 1/4 inch from the top of the mamenori (this is to seal the roll). Lay a quarter of the mesclun across the bottom two-thirds of the mamenori. Add a quarter of the crab mixture, mango, peanuts, cilantro, and cucumber across the bottom third, keeping some peanuts, cilantro, and cucumber aside for garnish. Roll firmly and seal. Repeat to make a total of 4 rolls.

Cut each roll into 4 pieces and place 4 pieces in the center of each of 4 plates. Ladle 2 tablespoons of the vinaigrette around the pieces. Dot with the chili sauce and scatter the remaining peanuts, cilantro, and cucumber over all.

Shrimp and Cream Cheese Wontons, Cucumber Salad, and Mango Coulis

Serves 4

The mango coulis makes this dish tropical. The colors—the deep, vibrant yellow of our local mangoes and cool green of the cucumber salad—make it beautiful. There's no reason to be intimidated by wonton wrapper folding—a little practice is all it takes. The main thing is not to overstuff.

MANGO COULIS

1/4 cup peeled and diced fresh mango

1/2 tablespoon rice vinegar

1/2 tablespoon freshly squeezed lemon juice

1/2 tablespoon mirin (sweet rice wine)

1/4 cup olive oil

Kosher salt and freshly ground black pepper

Sweet Thai chili sauce

1 cup cream cheese, softened

1 teaspoon chopped fresh basil

1 teaspoon chopped fresh cilantro

1 teaspoon chopped fresh chives

2 teaspoons freshly squeezed lemon juice

2 teaspoons masago (smelt roe)

Kosher salt and freshly ground black pepper

8 extra-large shrimp, peeled and deveined, tail on

8 (2 by 2-inch) wonton wrappers

1 egg, lightly beaten

Cottonseed, peanut, or canola oil for deep-frying

1 cup julienned Japanese cucumber

1 cup julienned carrot

1 cup julienned daikon radish

To prepare the coulis, in a blender, combine the mango, vinegar, lemon juice, and mirin. Blend until pureed. With the motor running, slowly add the olive oil, blending until thickened. Season with salt and pepper and sweet Thai chili sauce to taste. The coulis can be made the night before and stored in an airtight container in the refrigerator.

In a small bowl, combine the cream cheese, basil, cilantro, chives, lemon juice, and masago. Season with salt and pepper. Season the shrimp with salt and pepper.

To prepare the wontons, on a clean, dry surface, lay the wonton wrappers. Position 1 shrimp in the center of each wrapper, leaving the tail sticking out of the wrapper. Place 2 teaspoons of the cheese mixture in the center of each shrimp. Brush the edges of the wrapper with the egg, fold to make a triangle, and seal. Repeat with the remaining wrappers.

In a heavy saucepan, pour in the oil to a depth of about 3 inches and heat to 375°. Add as many wontons as will fit without overcrowding and fry, turning with tongs to cook evenly, until crisp and golden brown, about 4 minutes. Using a wire-mesh skimmer or slotted metal spoon, transfer to paper towels to drain. Repeat with the remaining wontons. Set aside.

In a bowl, combine the cucumber, carrot, and daikon. Place a small mound of the vegetables on each of 4 plates. Top each mound with 2 wontons. Spoon 2 tablespoons of coulis onto the wontons and vegetables and around the plate. Serve.

Japanese Calamari Salad

This is my wife's all-time favorite Sansei dish. We love Kochujang dressing but realized it might be too spicy for some people. So we played around with this dish, adapting it to more palates, and it's been a signature item at the restaurant ever since. Kochujang pepper, by the way, is a Korean chili powder, which comes in small tins or in bricks in its paste form. It's available in Korean markets, or you could substitute Mexican achiote paste or even ancho chili powder.

KOCHUJANG DRESSING

6 tablespoons Kochujang pepper

1/2 cup sugar

1/2 cup rice vinegar

2/3 cup peanut oil

Kosher salt

Cottonseed, peanut, or canola oil for deep-frying

4 (6 by 6-inch) wonton wrappers

CALAMARI SALAD

1 pound calamari tubes and tentacles, cleaned

Kosher salt and freshly ground black pepper

1 cup all-purpose flour

2 cups mesclun (mixed salad greens)

1 teaspoon black sesame seeds, for garnish

1 teaspoon white sesame seeds, for garnish

1 teaspoon chopped fresh chives, for garnish

4 lemon wedges

To prepare the dressing, in a blender, combine the Kochujang pepper, sugar, and vinegar and blend until smooth. Kochujang pepper is very coarse, so it may take a while to make it smooth. With the motor running, slowly add the oil, blending until thickened. Season with salt. The dressing should be the consistency of ketchup. It can be prepared up to 2 weeks ahead of time and stored in an airtight container in the refrigerator.

(continued)

continued from page 109

To prepare the wonton baskets, in a large saucepan, pour in the oil to a depth of about 6 inches and heat to 375°. Press each wrapper around the outside of a large ladle or a bowl until it takes on its shape. One at a time, add a wrapper to the oil and fry until golden brown and crisp, about 2 minutes per wrapper. Using a slotted metal spoon or fine-mesh sieve, transfer to paper towels to drain. Set aside. Reserve the oil.

To prepare the salad, cut the calamari tubes crosswise into ½-inch pieces. Season with salt and pepper. Toss the calamari in the flour to evenly coat, shaking off the excess. Return the oil to 375°. Add the calamari in batches, frying until crisp, 2 to 3 minutes per batch. Using a slotted spoon, transfer to paper towels to drain. In a bowl, toss the calamari in the Kochujang dressing.

To assemble the salad, place ¼ cup of the greens on each of 4 plates. Place 1 wonton basket on top of the greens. Pile another ¼ cup of greens inside each basket. Fill each basket with the calamari and top with a few black and white sesame seeds. Sprinkle the chives over all and serve with a lemon wedge on the side.

Poached Keahole Lobster Salad Of Waimanalo Micro Greens, Strawberry Papaya, and Creamy Tarragon Vinaigrette

Serves 4

This is a great summer salad—cool and refreshing. Our fresh upcountry greens and fresh local strawberry papaya are the perfect counterpoints to the sweet Kona Maine lobster. Waimanalo has very fertile soil, not as acidic as, say, Kula, and produces beautiful and mild-flavored produce. Strawberry papaya is a sweeter and more colorful variety than the regular papaya. We also like to use it for its texture, which is a little firmer and holds up better in this type of usage. The lobsters arrive as one-inch fledgelings from Maine and are raised to maturity in refrigerated, cold-water ponds at Keahole (near Kona) on the island of Hawai'i. I add some tarragon because the flavor is very complementary to lobster.

CREAMY TARRAGON VINAIGRETTE

¹/₄ tablespoon Dijon mustard

1 teaspoon sugar

5 tablespoons rice wine vinegar

¹/₄ teaspoon minced shallot

¹/₂ cup grapeseed or canola oil

¹/₄ cup finely chopped fresh tarragon

Kosher salt and freshly ground black pepper

2 (1¹/₂-pound) Maine lobsters, cooked

Kosher salt and freshly ground black pepper

4 cups micro greens

2 cups thinly sliced strawberry papaya or other papaya

¹/₂ cup slivered Maui onion or other sweet onion

1 cup kaiware sprouts

1 tablespoon black sesame seeds, for garnish

1 tablespoon white sesame seeds, for garnish

(continued)

continued from page 111

To prepare the vinaigrette, in a glass or stainless steel bowl, whisk together the mustard, sugar, vinegar, and shallot. Slowly whisk in the oil until the mixture thickens. Mix in the tarragon and season with salt and pepper. Chill slightly before using.

Split the lobsters in half and season with salt and pepper.

To serve, place a mound of greens in the center of each of 4 plates. Arrange the papaya slices around the greens. Place half a lobster tail and one claw on top of the greens. Sprinkle the onions and sprouts on top of the lobster. Drizzle the tarragon vinaigrette over the greens and lobster and sprinkle the black and white sesame seeds over all.

Scallop and Foie Gras Nigiri, Caramelized Granny Smith Apples, and Unagi Sauce

Serves 4

Nigiri means fish on top of rice. This is foie gras on top of scallop. What could be better? The apples add both a sweet and a tart element, complementing the buttery richness of the foie gras.

1 cup diced Granny Smith apple

2 teaspoons unsalted butter

1 tablespoon sugar

4 large sea scallops

4 ounces grade A foie gras, deveined and sliced into 4 pieces

Kosher salt and freshly ground black pepper

4 (1 by 5-inch) strips nori (dried seaweed)

4 teaspoons Unagi Sauce (page 89)

In a large sauté pan over medium-high heat, sauté the apple in 1 teaspoon of the butter until tender, 3 to 4 minutes. Add the remaining 1 teaspoon butter and the sugar and cook, stirring, until the sugar turns a golden brown, about 5 minutes. Set aside and let cool.

Season the scallops and foie gras with salt and pepper. In a skillet, add the scallops and foie gras and sear over high heat until golden brown, 2 to 3 minutes per side.

To assemble the nigiri, place a piece of foie gras on top of each scallop and wrap each with 1 nori strip to keep the foie gras in place. To serve, arrange the 4 nigiri on the center of a platter. Spoon the apples and drizzle the unagi sauce around the nigiri.

Scallop and Truffle Ravioli, Enoki Mushrooms, and Yuzu Butter Sauce

Serves 4

We created this dish just before Christmas 2001, when winter black truffle season was at its peak. We were testing different dishes using truffles and scallops, a good combination because the earthiness of the truffles brings out the sweetness of the scallops. I love bringing in the truffles each winter because it gives our other chefs the opportunity to work with exotic ingredients. Canned truffles are fine, but of course if you can get fresh it's even better.

4 bunches baby bok choy

1 tablespoon unsalted butter

Kosher salt and freshly ground black pepper

8 (4 by 4-inch) wonton wrappers

4 large day boat or sea scallops

1 large black truffle, thinly sliced

1 egg, lightly beaten

1 cup Yuzu Butter Sauce (page 87)

1 cup enoki mushrooms, trimmed, or other wild mushrooms, sliced

4 teaspoons flying fish roe (tobiko), for garnish

In a sauté pan over medium-high heat, sauté the bok choy in the butter until tender, 3 to 4 minutes. Season with salt and pepper. Keep warm.

Bring a large pot of water to a boil. Meanwhile, on a clean, dry surface, lay the wonton wrappers. Place 1 scallop in the center of each wrapper and top each scallop with a quarter of the truffle slices. Place a second wrapper on top. Brush the edges of 1 wrapper with the egg and seal. Repeat with the remaining wrappers to make 4 ravioli. Place the ravioli in the boiling water and cook until tender, about 3 minutes.

To serve, place a quarter of the bok choy in the center of each of 4 plates and top each with 1 ravioli. Ladle the warm sauce around the ravioli. Top each with a quarter of the mushrooms and dot each plate with 1 teaspoon of the tobiko. Serve immediately.

Rock Shrimp and Spicy Crab Lumpia with Yuzu Butter and Unagi Glaze

Serves 4

Every culture has a "wrapper": Chinese wontons, Italian ravioli, Filipino lumpia, for example. We chose lumpia for this dish because of its softer texture; lumpia wrappers can be found in many Asian markets. We prepared this dish for the first time for an event at the Honolulu Academy of Arts. It proves one of my basic theories: Fried seafood served with a great sauce is always a hit.

$^1/_2$ cup rock shrimp, blanched

1 cup Spicy Crab Mix (page 77)

2 tablespoons chopped fresh cilantro

4 lumpia wrappers

1 egg, lightly beaten

1 cup cornstarch

Cottonseed, peanut, or canola oil for deep-frying

2 cups Yuzu Butter Sauce (page 87)

1 cup Unagi Sauce (page 89)

$^1/_2$ cup micro greens

In a saucepot, bring 3 cups of salted water to a boil. Add the shrimp and cook, stirring constantly, for 3 minutes, until the shrimp are just opaque and starting to turn pink and firm. Drain, then immerse in ice water to stop the cooking process and preserve the texture. Transfer the shrimp to a bowl and combine with the crab mix and cilantro.

On a clean, dry surface, lay the lumpia wrappers so they are diamond-shaped facing you. Place 3 tablespoons of the crab mixture 3 inches from the bottom of each wrapper. Cover the filling with the point at the bottom. Bring the left point into the center and then the right point into the center. Brush the edges of the wrapper with the egg and seal. Roll each wrapper in cornstarch to evenly coat. Repeat with the remaining wrappers.

In a heavy saucepan, pour in the oil to a depth of about 4 inches and heat to 350°. Add the lumpia and fry, turning with tongs to cook evenly, until golden brown, about 3 minutes. Using a slotted spoon, transfer to paper towels to drain. To serve, ladle the yuzu sauce onto each of 4 plates. Cut each lumpia in half diagonally. Place both halves on each plate and drizzle the unagi sauce over all. Top the lumpia with the greens. Serve immediately.

Ravioli of Nori, Rock Shrimp, Crab, and Lobster

Serves 4

For me, this is the ultimate luxury dish. It's great seafood in a better-tasting wrapper than pasta because it's "eggier." Add in the sauce with the fresh shiitake mushrooms, and *wow!*

TRUFFLE MADEIRA CREAM SAUCE

2 cups Madeira wine

2 cups heavy cream

1/2 cup Veal Demi-Glace (page 95)

1/2 cup sliced fresh shiitake mushrooms

2 tablespoons Truffle Butter (page 93)

1 cup chopped rock shrimp

2 tablespoons chopped crabmeat

1/2 cup chopped lobster meat

1 tablespoon diced Maui onion or other sweet onion

1/2 tablespoon chopped fresh tarragon

12 (2 by 2-inch) wonton wrappers

12 (1-inch-square) pieces nori (dried seaweed)

1 egg, lightly beaten

1 tablespoon chopped fresh chives, for garnish

To make the cream sauce, in a saucepan, add the wine and cook over high heat to reduce by half, about 8 minutes. Add the cream and cook to reduce by a quarter, about 8 minutes. Add the demi-glace, reduce the heat to medium-low, and simmer for 20 minutes. Remove from the heat, add the mushrooms, and gently whisk in the truffle butter until smooth. Keep warm.

In a large bowl, mix the shrimp, crab, lobster, onion, and tarragon. To assemble the ravioli, on a clean, dry surface, lay the wonton wrappers. Place 1 nori in the center of each wrapper. Place 1 tablespoon of the shrimp mixture in the center of each nori. Brush the edges with the egg, fold the wrapper into a rectangle, and seal. Make sure the ravioli is completely sealed so the filling won't seep out during cooking.

In a large pot, bring 1 gallon of salted water to a boil. Decrease the heat to medium and add the ravioli to the water. Simmer for 5 to 6 minutes, until the ravioli is tender. Drain. To serve, place 3 ravioli in each of 4 bowls. Ladle the cream sauce over the ravioli and top with the chives. Serve.

Lobster and Pork Hash Dumplings, Cucumber Sunomono Salad, and Sesame-Soy Dipping Sauce

Serves 6

This dish is a nontraditional dim sum that we love to serve at the restaurant as a first course. The dipping sauce is spicy, which boosts up the lobster meat and the pork. The cucumber sunomono salad adds the Sansei touch.

CUCUMBER SUNOMONO SALAD

1 pound Japanese cucumber, halved lengthwise and thinly sliced

1/4 cup kosher salt

1/2 cup rice vinegar

1/4 cup sugar

1 teaspoon shoyu (Japanese soy sauce)

1/4 cup slivered Maui onion or other sweet onion

1/4 cup julienned carrot

SESAME-SOY DIPPING SAUCE

1/2 cup shoyu (Japanese soy sauce)

1 tablespoon Asian (toasted) sesame oil

1/8 teaspoon white sesame seeds, toasted (page 16)

1 tablespoon rice vinegar

1/8 teaspoon sambal (Indonesian chili paste)

1 (8-ounce) lobster tail, meat removed and diced

8 ounces ground pork

2 tablespoons minced water chestnuts

2 teaspoons finely chopped green onion, green part only

1 teaspoon minced garlic

1/2 tablespoon peeled and minced fresh ginger

Kosher salt and freshly ground black pepper

18 (2 by 2-inch) wonton wrappers

1 egg, lightly beaten

Cottonseed, peanut, or canola oil for deep-frying

To prepare the sunomono, in a large bowl, combine the cucumber and salt. Let stand for 15 minutes, then rinse the cucumber well. Rinse the bowl well, then return the cucumber to the bowl and add the vinegar, sugar, shoyu, onion, and carrot. Marinate in the refrigerator for at least 1 hour and keep chilled until ready to use.

To prepare the dipping sauce, in a small bowl, combine the shoyu, oil, sesame seeds, vinegar, and sambal. Cover and let sit at room temperature for at least 1 hour before serving.

To prepare the filling, in a bowl, combine the lobster, pork, water chestnuts, green onion, garlic, and ginger. Season with salt and pepper.

To prepare the dumplings, on a clean, dry surface, lay the wonton wrappers. Spoon ½ tablespoon of the lobster mixture into the center of each wrapper. Brush the edges with the egg, fold the wrappers into triangles, and seal well. In a heavy saucepan, pour in the oil to a depth of about 2 inches and heat to 375°. Add the wontons and fry, turning with tongs to cook evenly, until golden brown, about 4 minutes. Using a slotted spoon, transfer to paper towels to drain.

To assemble, divide the cucumber salad among 6 plates and place in the center of each plate. Arrange 3 dumplings each around the salad. Serve with the dipping sauce on the side.

Asian Rock Shrimp Cake with Ginger-Lime-Chili Butter

Serves 4

Our first award winner! We needed a must-try, must-have dish when we first opened the restaurant. Crab cakes were overdone, so we said, "Let's do a shrimp cake," and we came up with this recipe. We dreamed up the ginger-lime-chili butter sauce within an hour of the first time we served the cake. Almost seven years later, it's still a must-have dish.

1 pound rock shrimp, peeled and coarsely chopped

1 egg

^{1}/$_3$ cup mayonnaise

^{1}/$_3$ cup fresh or canned bamboo shoots, cut into ^{1}/$_4$-inch strips

^{1}/$_4$ cup finely chopped green onion, green part only

^{1}/$_2$ teaspoon freshly squeezed lemon juice

^{1}/$_8$ teaspoon Tabasco sauce

Pinch of freshly ground black pepper

1 ^{3}/$_4$ cups panko (Japanese breadcrumbs)

4 ounces Chinese egg noodles

Cottonseed, peanut, or canola oil for deep-frying

1 cup Ginger-Lime-Chili Butter Sauce (page 85)

Squeeze the rock shrimp to remove excess moisture. In a large bowl, combine the shrimp, egg, mayonnaise, bamboo shoots, green onion, lemon juice, Tabasco sauce, and pepper, mixing well. Form the mixture into 4 patties. Turn each patty in the panko to coat evenly. Wrap a quarter of the noodles around each patty. In a heavy saucepan, pour in the oil to a depth of about 4 inches and heat to 360°. Add the patties and fry, turning with tongs to cook evenly, until the noodles are crunchy and golden brown, 3 to 4 minutes. Using a slotted spoon, transfer to paper towels to drain.

To serve, spoon the sauce on each of 4 plates and top with 1 shrimp cake each. Serve immediately.

Rock Shrimp Dynamite

Serves 6

One night, we found out that our publicist, after working with us for almost four years, had never tasted this signature dish. Now, we just bring her a plate whenever she walks in the door. She says it's like eating candy for her first course.

Cottonseed, peanut, or canola oil for deep-frying

6 (2 by 2-inch) wonton wrappers

3 cups rock shrimp

2 cups all-purpose flour

5 cups tempura batter

2 cups Masago Aioli (page 76)

4 cups loosely packed Nalo greens or other mixed greens

3/4 cup Unagi Sauce (page 89)

6 tablespoons finely chopped green onion, green part only, for garnish

1/2 cup white sesame seeds, for garnish

In a heavy saucepan, pour in the oil to a depth of about 4 inches and heat to 350°. Add the wonton wrappers and fry, turning with tongs to cook evenly, until golden brown and crisp, about 3 minutes. Using a slotted spoon, transfer to paper towels to drain. Set aside. Reserve the oil.

Toss the shrimp in the flour to coat evenly, shaking off the excess. Return the oil to 350°. In batches, dip the shrimp into the tempura batter to coat completely, then transfer to the oil and fry until golden brown, 3 to 4 minutes. Using a slotted spoon, transfer to paper towels to drain. Toss the shrimp in a bowl with the masago aioli to evenly coat.

To assemble, place a pile of greens on each of 6 plates, and top with 1 wonton each. Place one-sixth of the shrimp on top of each wonton. Drizzle each with the unagi sauce and top with the green onion and sesame seeds. Serve immediately.

Miso Garlic
Monster Black Tiger Prawns

Serves 4

This is our version of Shrimp Scampi. The miso gives this dish its saltiness and a little more flavor than the traditional version. We also broil the prawns instead of sautéing them. Black tiger prawns—"colossal" in size—come from Southeast Asia. They're clean and sweet, and we love to use them in this dish.

12 black tiger prawns, peeled and deveined

1/2 teaspoon kosher salt

1 tablespoon sugar

1/2 cup unsalted butter, at room temperature

1 tablespoon chopped garlic

2 tablespoons white miso (soybean paste)

2 tablespoons panko (Japanese breadcrumbs)

2 cups mesclun (mixed salad greens)

2 tablespoons Umeboshi Vinaigrette (page 92)

Preheat the broiler. To butterfly the prawns, slice each prawn lengthwise from the underside without cutting all the way through, then open up so the prawn can lie flat. In a bowl, combine the salt and sugar with 2 cups water and mix until the salt and sugar are dissolved. Add the prawns to the mixture and marinate for 10 minutes.

In another bowl, mix the butter, garlic, and miso until well combined. Remove the prawns from the marinade and pat dry. Spread 1/2 teaspoon of the miso mixture over each prawn. Sprinkle the panko evenly on the prawns and transfer to a baking sheet. Broil the prawns for 3 minutes, or until they are brown and slightly crisp on the outside.

To assemble, place 1/2 cup of the greens on each of 4 plates and drizzle 1/2 tablespoon of the vinaigrette over the greens. Place 3 prawns on each pile of greens. Serve immediately.

Chili and Sake–Glazed Deepwater Prawns

Serves 4 to 6

The combination of the chilies, freshly grated green papaya, and sake is a beautiful balance of flavors that goes very well with the texture and sweetness of the deepwater prawns. That combination also helps to enhance the richness of the flavor in the heads of the prawns. Yes, folks, you "suck" out the heads of the prawns when you eat this dish. Green papaya (also called cooking papaya) is a varietal used most often in Thai and Vietnamese cooking; it's not an unripe regular papaya.

SWEET THAI CHILI MARINADE

1/4 cup sweet Thai chili sauce

1 tablespoon rice vinegar

1/4 cup sake

1/2 teaspoon red Thai curry paste

GREEN PAPAYA SALAD

2 green papayas, peeled, seeded, and coarsely grated (about 3 1/2 cups)

1/2 cup loosely packed fresh cilantro leaves

1 medium-size red jalapeño pepper, seeded and cut into 1/2-inch strips

Kosher salt and freshly ground black pepper

WASABI LOBSTER SAUCE

2 cups lobster stock (page 94)

1/4 cup wasabi paste

1/4 cup rice vinegar

1/4 cup mirin (sweet rice wine)

1/4 cup sake

1 cup unsalted butter, at room temperature

12 colossal shrimp, peeled and deveined, heads on

Fresh cilantro sprigs, for garnish

Prepare a fire in a charcoal grill or preheat a gas grill.

To prepare the marinade, in a small stainless steel bowl, whisk together the chili sauce, vinegar, sake, and curry paste. Let stand for 10 minutes. Cover and refrigerate until ready to use.

To prepare the salad, in a large bowl, toss the papaya, cilantro, and jalapeño with half of the marinade. Season with salt and pepper. Cover and chill for at least 10 minutes to allow the flavors to combine.

To make the sauce, in a saucepan, bring the stock to a simmer over medium heat. Add the wasabi, vinegar, mirin, and sake and cook until the mixture is reduced by half, about 8 minutes. Remove from the heat and whisk in the butter until smooth. Keep warm.

In a large bowl, toss the prawns with the remaining half of the marinade. Grill the prawns until they just begin to curl and turn pink, about 4 minutes per side.

To assemble, divide the green papaya salad evenly among the plates. Arrange 2 to 3 prawns around the salad and drizzle the sauce around the plate. Garnish each with a cilantro sprig.

Seared Miso Scallops with Furikake Rice Cake, Baby Nalo Greens, and Sweet Miso Sauce

Serves 4

This is the perfect way to infuse flavor into not-so-flavorful scallops. I believe we were the first restaurant ever to do this. We tried it out at the Winter Wine Escape, an annual Island of Hawai'i food festival. Attendees loved it!

12 large day boat or sea scallops

1 cup Miso Marinade (page 96)

2 cups cooked short- or medium-grain white rice

2 tablespoons furikake (rice seasoning)

1 tablespoon finely chopped green onion, green part only

Kosher salt and freshly ground black pepper

1 tablespoon cottonseed, peanut, or canola oil

1/2 cup loosely packed baby Nalo or other baby greens

1/2 cup Su-Miso Sauce (page 88)

1 tablespoon flying fish roe (tobiko), for garnish

3 shiso (perilla) leaves, cut into chiffonade, for garnish (optional)

In a bowl, combine the scallops with the marinade. Cover and chill for at least 1 hour, but no longer than 4 hours.

Meanwhile, to prepare the rice cakes, in a small bowl, combine the rice, furikake, and green onion. Season with salt and pepper. Divide the rice mixture and, using a nigiri sushi mold or small bowl, form into 4 rice cakes. Remove from the mold and set aside.

Heat the oil in a nonstick skillet over high heat. Add the scallops and sear for about 2 minutes per side, until the scallops are light golden brown.

To assemble, place 1 rice cake in the center of each of 4 plates. Place 3 scallops around the rice cake, top with the greens, and drizzle the su-miso sauce on top. Garnish with the tobiko and shiso chiffonade, if using. Serve.

Tempura-Fried Nori-Wrapped Scallop Mousse with Wasabi Cream

Serves 4

Another fusion of classical French (in the form of the mousse) with Asian comfort food (in the form of the nori and the technique of tempura frying).

WASABI CREAM

- 1/4 cup wasabi paste
- 1 teaspoon mirin (sweet rice wine)
- 1 tablespoon olive oil

- 1 pound scallops
- 1 egg
- 1 cup heavy cream
- Kosher salt and freshly ground black pepper

- 2 sheets nori (dried seaweed), cut in half lengthwise
- Cottonseed, peanut, or canola oil for deep-frying
- 1/4 cup flour
- 1 cup tempura batter
- 1/4 cup gari (pickled ginger), for garnish
- 1/4 cup kaiware sprouts, for garnish

To prepare the wasabi cream, in a bowl, mix together the wasabi and mirin. Slowly whisk in the oil until smooth. Adjust the flavor with rice vinegar or water to your taste. Set aside.

To prepare the mousse, in a food processor, process the scallops until smooth, about 4 minutes. Add the egg and cream and process until light and fluffy, about 1 minute. Be careful not to overprocess, or the heat from the processor will cook the ingredients. Season with salt and pepper.

On a clean, dry surface, place 1 half sheet nori, shiny-side down and with the long side closest to you. Spread a quarter of the mousse across the end closest to you. Rolling away from you, roll the nori over the filling. Wet the top inside edge of the nori with water and seal the roll. The resulting roll should be about 1½ inches in diameter. Repeat with the remaining nori and mousse to make a total of 4 rolls.

In a wok or heavy, deep skillet, pour in the oil to a depth of 4 inches and heat to 350°. Turn the rolls in the flour to coat evenly, shaking off the excess, then dip them in the tempura batter to coat completely. Add to the wok and fry until the nori is crisp, 3 to 4 minutes. Using a slotted spoon, transfer to paper towels to drain.

To serve, slice each roll into 5 pieces and arrange the pieces on 4 plates. Top with the gari and sprouts. Serve with the wasabi cream on the side.

Blue Crab Soufflé

Serves 4

This is like crab au gratin, only richer and better.

2 tablespoons unsalted butter	Kosher salt and freshly ground black pepper
1/2 cup julienned Maui onion or other sweet onion	2 cups sliced Yukon Gold potatoes
1 tablespoon chopped garlic	2 cups cooked blue crabmeat
2 cups heavy cream	8 tablespoons freshly grated Parmesan cheese

Preheat the oven to 350°. In a saucepan, heat the butter over medium heat. Add the onion and garlic, reduce the heat to low, and cook, uncovered, for 2 minutes, until translucent. The onion and garlic should not brown. Add the cream and reduce the mixture by one-fourth, 10 to 12 minutes. Season with salt and pepper.

In 4 individual ceramic ramekins or soufflé cups, spoon about 1½ tablespoons of the cream mixture. Divide the potato into 8 portions and add 1 portion to each ramekin, then add ¼ cup of the crabmeat to each. Repeat the layers. Top each with 2 tablespoons Parmesan cheese. Bake for about 10 minutes, or until bubbling and golden brown. Serve immediately.

Asian Steamed Clams

Serves 4

This is a particularly rich clam dish because, of course, of the butter. We add a touch of black bean, a touch of spice (the sambal) and some Asian herbs (Thai basil and cilantro). People like it so much, they actually pick up their bowls in the restaurant and drink the broth. When buying hard-shell clams like Manila, select only the ones that are closed, and be sure to rinse them well.

3 tablespoons fermented black soybeans (not turtle beans)

1 tablespoon cottonseed, peanut, or canola oil

2 tablespoons chopped garlic

1 pound Manila clams

$1/4$ cup sake

3/4 cup chicken stock

2 tablespoons chiffonade of fresh Thai basil

$1/4$ cup diced red tomato

$1/4$ cup diced yellow tomato

1 teaspoon sambal (Indonesian chili paste)

3 tablespoons unsalted butter

Kosher salt and freshly ground black pepper

4 fresh cilantro sprigs, for garnish

Rinse the beans for about 5 minutes in cold water; drain. In a skillet, heat the oil over medium-high heat. Add the the garlic and black beans and sauté for 2 minutes. Add the clams, sake, and stock and cook until the alcohol cooks off, about 2 minutes. Cover and cook until the clams open, 2 to 3 minutes. Add the Thai basil, red and yellow tomato, sambal, and butter and stir to combine. Remove from the heat and let stand, covered, for 5 minutes. Season with salt and pepper.

To serve, divide the clams and broth among 4 bowls. Top each with 1 cilantro sprig.

Steamed Manila Clams, Soba Noodles, Enoki Mushrooms, and Lobster Miso Broth

Serves 4

Everyone, everyone, everyone in Hawaiʻi eats saimin—and it works for breakfast, lunch, and dinner. It's the local "chicken noodle soup." Traditionally, it's a pork-based broth with noodles, a little green onion, and maybe some meat or fish cake. This is Chef Keith's version of "fancy" saimin. Plum wine is readily available in Asian markets.

1 whole Maine lobster	¹/₄ cup white miso (soybean paste)
2 tablespoons plus 1 teaspoon cottonseed, peanut, or canola oil	2 teaspoons hondashi (Japanese soup base)
¹/₄ cup finely diced carrot	1 pound soba (buckwheat noodles)
¹/₄ cup finely diced onion	2 pounds Manila clams
1 tablespoon minced garlic	2 cups enoki mushrooms, trimmed
1 cup plum wine	1 cup julienned bok choy

To prepare the broth, remove the lobster head and, using a large French chef's knife or a cleaver, coarsely chop. Remove the meat from the body and tail and set aside. In a medium stockpot, heat 2 tablespoons of the oil over high heat, add the lobster head, carrot, onion, and garlic, and sauté until brown, about 7 minutes. Add the plum wine, reduce the heat to medium, and cook to reduce by half, about 3 minutes. Add 5 cups water, the miso, and hondashi and simmer for 10 minutes. Strain the liquid through a fine-mesh sieve; set aside.

Cook the noodles as directed on the package. Fill a bowl with ice water. Transfer the noodles to the ice water to stop the cooking process; drain. Set aside.

In a sauté pan, heat the remaining 1 teaspoon oil over medium heat. Add the clams and sauté for 2 minutes. Add the broth, mushrooms, bok choy, and lobster meat and simmer until all the clams have opened, about 5 minutes. Divide the noodles among 4 serving bowls and top with the clams, lobster, and vegetables. Serve immediately.

Roasted Botan Ebi with Chow Fun and Sambal Sauce

Serves 4

We emphasize "family style" at Sansei. This is an excellent example of a dish that everyone can and does share. Crown Noodle in Honolulu specially makes the chow fun we use at the restaurant. When preparing this dish, use the freshest noodles available in your area. Dry noodles work, too, so no worries. This dish is true, local-style comfort food; it's very spicy, but everyone in Hawai'i, even kids, love spicy. This one gets four stars!

6 tablespoons cottonseed, peanut, or canola oil

2 tablespoons minced garlic

2 tablespoons peeled and minced fresh ginger

1/4 cup rice vinegar

2 tablespoons sambal (Indonesian chili paste)

1/2 cup sweet Thai chili sauce

2 tablespoons sugar (optional)

2 large carrots, cut into julienne

4 medium yellow onions, cut into julienne

2 pounds fresh or dried chow fun noodles, cooked

1/4 cup coarsely chopped peanuts

1 cup chopped fresh cilantro

20 extra-large shrimp, peeled and deveined

1/2 cup water chestnuts

1/4 cup chopped fresh Thai basil, for garnish

1/4 cup finely chopped green onion, green part only, for garnish

To prepare the sauce, in a skillet, heat 2 tablespoons of the oil over high heat. Add the garlic and ginger and sauté for 1 minute. Add the vinegar and stir to loosen any of the caramelized pieces of garlic and ginger in the pan. Add the sambal and chili sauce and stir to combine. Add up to 2 tablespoons sugar, if desired, to adjust the flavor; mix well. Transfer the mixture to a bowl and set aside. Clean the skillet to use again.

In a wok or heavy, deep skillet, heat 2 tablespoons of the oil over medium-high heat. Sauté the carrots and onions until tender, about 8 minutes. Add the chow fun and stir to combine. Add the sambal sauce, reserving 1 tablespoon, and stir to mix well. Add two-thirds of the peanuts and cilantro, tossing to combine. Set aside.

In a skillet, heat the remaining 2 tablespoons oil over medium heat. Add the shrimp and water chestnuts and sauté until the shrimp just begin to curl and turn pink, 5 to 6 minutes. Add the reserved sambal sauce, stirring to combine.

To serve, transfer the noodles to a large platter. Arrange the shrimp mixture on top of the noodles. Top with the remaining peanuts and cilantro, the Thai basil, and green onion. Serve immediately.

Sansei Surf 'n' Turf

Serves 4

Gotta have surf 'n' turf! Since we're the "home of the other red meat," the ahi is the turf and the sweet shrimp (we use Kaua'i shrimp), lightly marinated, is the surf. We serve it with sweet miso and Gorgonzola cheese. It sounds odd, I know, but you've gotta try it.

4 pieces extra-large sweet shrimp (amaebi), heads on

1 teaspoon kosher salt

1 tablespoon sugar

4 tablespoons cottonseed, peanut, or canola oil, plus additional for deep-frying

1 teaspoon chopped garlic

2 cups loosely packed baby tatsoi or baby bok choy

Kosher salt and freshly ground black pepper

4 (1-ounce) pieces sashimi-grade ahi

1/2 cup cornstarch

1 cup Su-Miso Sauce (page 88)

3 tablespoons Gorgonzola cheese, crumbled

1/4 cup chopped macadamia nuts

1/4 cup loosely packed micro greens

In a bowl, combine the shrimp, salt, and sugar. Add enough water to cover. Set aside for 5 minutes, then drain. Remove the heads from the shrimp and reserve both heads and bodies.

In a sauté pan, heat 1 tablespoon of the oil over medium-high heat. Add the garlic and tatsoi and sauté until wilted, about 4 minutes. Season with salt and pepper. Set aside.

Season the ahi with salt and pepper. In a skillet, heat 1 tablespoon of the oil over medium-high heat. Add the ahi and sear until medium-rare, 1 to 2 minutes per side, until slightly white around the edges. Set aside.

In a small skillet, heat 2 tablespoons of the oil over medium-high heat. Add the shrimp and sauté until the shrimp just begin to curl and turn pink, about 3 minutes. Set aside.

Toss the shrimp heads in the cornstarch to coat evenly, shaking off the excess. In a heavy saucepan, pour in the oil to a depth of about 3 inches and heat to 350°. Add the shrimp heads and fry, turning with tongs to cook evenly, until crisp, 3 to 4 minutes. Using a slotted spoon, transfer to paper towels to drain. Set aside.

To assemble, divide the tatsoi and place in the center of each of 4 plates. Place 1 piece of ahi each on the tatsoi. Drizzle the sauce over the ahi. Sprinkle the cheese and nuts on top. Place 1 shrimp on top of each, then top with 1 shrimp head. Scatter micro greens over all and serve.

Seared Ahi Tataki Salad

Serves 4

This salad is so good, so nice, so light, so delicious—in other words, it's a great summer dish. Tataki refers to the cooking technique of seasoning and searing on all sides to caramelize, leaving the inside cool and rare, then slicing across to show the rare inside and caramelized outside.

1 tablespoon cottonseed, peanut, or canola oil

12 ounces sashimi-grade ahi (about 10 by 4 by 1 inch)

1/2 tablespoon grated daikon radish

Pinch of cayenne pepper

2 teaspoons smelt roe (masago)

1 tablespoon finely chopped green onion, green part only

1 teaspoon kaiware sprouts

1/2 cup slivered Maui onion or other sweet onion

2 tablespoons dried wakame (seaweed), rehydrated

1/4 cup Ponzu Sauce (page 82)

1 teaspoon white sesame seeds, for garnish

In a large sauté pan, heat the oil over high heat. Add the ahi and sear on each of its 4 sides for 10 seconds per side. It will be rare. Transfer to a clean cutting board and cut into 24 thin slices. In a small mixing bowl, prepare momiji oroshi by combining the daikon and cayenne pepper (more cayenne can be added if desired). Add the smelt roe, green onion, sprouts, onion, wakame, and sauce and combine. Add the ahi and gently toss. To serve, divide the mixture evenly among 4 small plates and top with the sesame seeds.

Panko-Crusted Ahi Sashimi with Soy-Wasabi Butter Sauce

Serves 4

I've seen different versions of this dish but none of them was exactly right. First of all, none of them had the right green—which is definitely arugula. Then, they needed the right crust—which we get from the panko. And, of course, it needed the right sauce. The texture comes from the roll; the flavor comes from the sauce. We use sashimi-grade ahi for this dish because the color of the tuna makes a big difference to the presentation.

2 sheets nori (dried seaweed), cut in half lengthwise

2 cups loosely packed baby spinach

2 cups loosely packed baby arugula

1/2 pound ahi, cut into 1-inch strips

Kosher salt and freshly ground black pepper

Cottonseed, peanut, or canola oil for deep-frying

1 cup all-purpose flour

1 1/2 cups tempura batter

2 cups panko (Japanese breadcrumbs)

3/4 cup Soy-Wasabi Butter Sauce (page 86)

1 teaspoon black sesame seeds, for garnish

1 teaspoon chopped fresh chives, for garnish

On a clean, dry surface, lay a nori, shiny-side down and with the long side closest to you. Cover each nori with a quarter of the spinach and arugula, leaving a 1/4-inch border at the top for sealing. Lay a quarter of the ahi strips across the center, season with salt and pepper, and roll tightly. Wet the inside edge of each nori with water and seal each roll.

In a heavy saucepan, pour in the oil to a depth of about 4 inches and heat to 375°. Coat the rolls with the flour, then dip in the tempura batter, then coat with the panko. Add the rolls to the oil and fry, turning with tongs to cook evenly, until golden brown, no more than 3 minutes. Using a slotted spoon, immediately remove the rolls from the oil and, handling carefully, slice each roll into 6 pieces; transfer to paper towels to drain. Be very careful not to overcook the roll, as the ahi in the center should be bright red and uncooked.

To serve, spoon 3 tablespoons sauce onto each of 4 plates and place 6 ahi roll pieces on top of the sauce. Sprinkle the sesame seeds and chives over all and serve immediately.

Broke-Down Poke Cakes with Wasabi Oil and Sweet Shoyu

Serves 4

This dish was an idea that came about in order to use the most scorned and, to my mind, most flavorful cuts of salmon (the belly) and ahi (side muscle), both of which contain a lot of fat. The result is an organized, clean presentation with great flavors that absorb the richness of the oils in the two fishes. During summer truffle season, treat yourself and shave a bit of white truffle on top of each cake. Sweet shoyu is a dark, dense, and delicious Indonesian sauce (where it is known as kecap manis); you can find it and wasabi oil at Asian markets.

1 pound sashimi-grade salmon, cut into ¼-inch dice

1 teaspoon white truffle oil

1 tablespoon fresh chervil

Kosher salt and freshly ground black pepper

3/4 pound sashimi-grade ahi steak, cut into ¼-inch dice

1 tablespoon minced Maui onion or other sweet onion

½ cup loosely packed arugula

4 tablespoons wasabi oil

4 tablespoons sweet shoyu (kecap manis)

8 ounces kaiware sprouts

In a stainless steel bowl, combine the salmon, truffle oil, and chervil. Season with salt and pepper. Be sure not to overmix, as this will cause the mixture to become cloudy. In another stainless steel bowl, combine the ahi and onion. Cover and chill both for 2 hours.

To assemble, layer a 3 by 3-inch ring mold (or 2-inch PVC pipe) with a quarter of the salmon (about 1 inch thick). Add a quarter of the arugula, then a quarter of the ahi. Unmold onto the center of a plate and drizzle with 1 tablespoon each of the wasabi oil and sweet shoyu. Top with a quarter of the sprouts. Repeat to make a total of 4 molds on 4 plates. Serve very cold.

Ahi Chutoro Tartare, Crispy Wonton Chips, Crème Fraîche, Wasabi Oil, and Beluga Caviar

Serves 4

Keith had something similar to this in San Francisco made with salmon. Since we have access to so much great local fresh fish here in Hawai'i, we decided to use the rich meat of the ahi. The addition of the crème fraîche and the caviar makes it even richer. This is a perfect dish for Sansei and so easy to make at home.

1 pound ahi chutoro (upper belly) or otoro (belly), minced

2 tablespoons finely chopped green onion, green part only

1 teaspoon Asian (toasted) sesame oil

1 tablespoon flying fish roe (tobiko)

Kosher salt and freshly ground black pepper

Cottonseed, peanut, or canola oil for deep-frying

8 (2 by 2-inch) wonton wrappers, cut into triangles

1/4 cup crème fraîche or sour cream

1 teaspoon beluga caviar, for garnish

1 teaspoon wasabi oil

In a small bowl, combine the tuna, green onion, sesame oil, and tobiko. Season with salt and pepper. Set aside.

In a heavy saucepan, pour in the oil to a depth of about 4 inches and heat to 375°. Add the wonton triangles and fry, turning with tongs to cook evenly, until golden brown, about 3 minutes. Using a slotted spoon, transfer to paper towels to drain. Let cool.

To assemble, place 1 tablespoon of the tuna mixture on each wonton chip. Top each with a dollop of crème fraîche and a little caviar. Arrange the chips on a platter, drizzle the wasabi oil over all, and serve.

Miso Butterfish

Talk about melt-in-your-mouth! It just doesn't get any better than this. This is a true test of Japanese cooking. If you can make a good miso butterfish and get the skin really crispy, then you've got a winner.

 4 (6-ounce) boneless butterfish fillets, skin on

 1 cup Miso Marinade (page 96)

 1/2 cup Su-Miso Sauce (page 88)

 1 cup chopped fresh chives, for garnish

 1 tablespoon shichimi (seven-spice pepper), for garnish

Place the butterfish fillets in a shallow dish and pour the marinade over them. Turn the fillets to coat well, cover, and refrigerate for at least 12 hours.

Preheat the oven to 400°. Remove the fillets from the marinade, shaking off the excess liquid, and transfer to a baking pan. Bake the fish until the skin is crispy, about 10 minutes. To serve, spoon 2 tablespoons of the sauce on each of 4 plates, and place 1 fillet on top of each. Sprinkle with the chives and shichimi. Serve.

Crispy Rice Paper-Wrapped Onaga, Foie Gras Mousse, and Ginger-Soy Broth

Serves 4

Keith's absolutely two favorite items with which to cook are our local long-tail red snapper, called onaga, and foie gras. They complement each other because of their richness. So rich, in fact, that we needed to make a light sauce to go with it and decided on the ginger-soy broth. Wrapping it in rice paper and frying it crisp adds a textural dimension. For this dish, be sure not to overprocess the mousse, because that will cook the foie gras and the natural fats will start to separate out of the mix. It is important to keep all of your ingredients well chilled.

FOIE GRAS MOUSSE

6 ounces grade A foie gras, deveined

1 egg yolk

2 teaspoons heavy cream

Kosher salt and freshly ground black pepper

4 sheets rice paper (summer roll wrappers)

12 ounces onaga or other snapper, cut into 4 pieces

Kosher salt and freshly ground black pepper

1 teaspoon plus ¹/₂ tablespoon cottonseed, peanut, or canola oil

1 teaspoon unsalted butter

4 bunches baby bok choy, cut in half lengthwise

1 cup diced fresh shiitake mushrooms

2 tablespoons peeled and minced fresh ginger

¹/₂ tablespoon minced garlic

4 cups chicken stock

2 tablespoons shoyu (Japanese soy sauce)

¹/₄ cup kaiware sprouts, for garnish

2 tablespoons white truffle oil, for garnish

To prepare the mousse, fill a large bowl with ice. In a food processor, process the foie gras until smooth, about 4 minutes. Add the egg yolk and heavy cream and process until the mixture becomes light and fluffy, about 2 minutes. Be careful not to overprocess, or the mixture will begin to separate. Season with salt and pepper. Quickly transfer the mousse to a bowl and place in the ice for a quick chill. Cover and refrigerate until the mousse starts to become firm, about 20 minutes.

Soak the rice paper in warm water until softened, about 3 minutes; drain. Transfer the wrappers to a clean, dry surface. Place 1 piece of snapper in the center of each wrapper and top each with a quarter of the mousse. Season with salt and pepper. Make an envelope out of each wrapper by folding the bottom toward the center, then folding the sides in and the top down over the folded sides. Press together to seal. Set aside for at least 10 minutes, to let the rice paper form a proper seal.

In a large skillet, heat 1 teaspoon of the oil over high heat. Add the snapper "packages," decrease the heat to medium-low, and sauté until both sides are golden brown, 3 to 4 minutes per side. Set aside.

In a sauté pan, heat the butter over high heat. Add the bok choy and sauté until wilted, about 3 minutes. Season with salt and pepper. Set aside.

To prepare the broth, in a saucepan set over low heat, add the mushrooms, ginger, garlic, and the remaining $\frac{1}{2}$ tablespoon of oil. Cook, uncovered, for 4 minutes. Add the stock and shoyu and cook to reduce the liquid by one-third, about 10 minutes. Keep warm.

To serve, divide the bok choy evenly among 4 large bowls. Top each with a snapper "package." Ladle the broth into each bowl and top each with sprouts and a drizzle of white truffle oil. Serve immediately.

Pacific Rim Lomilomi Salmon with Wonton Chips

Serves 4

When I was in Aspen, I craved Hawaiian food. We didn't have any salted salmon, typically used in lomilomi salmon. So we had to use fresh sushi salmon to make this dish. I think it tastes so much better our way, because the buttery nature of the salmon really comes through. We add a crispy wonton for "da crunch."

8 ounces sashimi-grade salmon, finely diced

1/4 cup extra virgin olive oil

1/4 cup julienned Maui onion or other sweet onion

1/4 cup seeded and diced tomato

1/4 cup chopped fresh cilantro

2 tablespoons finely chopped green onion, green part only

1 tablespoon kosher salt

1 tablespoon sambal (Indonesian chili paste)

8 (2 by 2-inch) wonton wrappers, cut into triangles

Cottonseed, peanut, or canola oil for deep-frying

1 tablespoon freshly squeezed lime juice

In a bowl, combine the salmon, olive oil, onion, tomato, cilantro, green onion, salt, and sambal and mix thoroughly. Cover and chill.

In a heavy saucepan, pour in the oil to a depth of about 4 inches and heat to 350°. Add as many wonton wrappers as will fit without overcrowding and fry, turning with tongs to cook evenly, until golden brown, about 3 minutes. Using a slotted spoon, transfer to paper towels to drain. Set aside.

To serve, stir the lime juice into the salmon mixture and transfer to a platter. Place the wonton chips around the edges and serve family-style. Let everyone dig in!

Sake-Cured Salmon Gravlax, Baby Mesclun, Crispy Salmon Skin, and Yuzu Vinaigrette

Serves 4

Keith loves gravlax, and this is his Asian version. The crispy salmon skin adds texture and the acidity of the yuzu really brings out the flavor of the gravlax.

YUZU VINAIGRETTE

- 1 tablespoon yuzu (Japanese citrus) juice or freshly squeezed lemon juice

- 2 1/2 teaspoons sugar

- 1 tablespoon rice vinegar

- 1/3 cup extra virgin olive oil

- Kosher salt and freshly ground black pepper

- 1 1/2 cups sake

- 1/2 cup sugar

- 1/2 cup kosher salt

- 1 bay leaf

- 1 cup finely chopped fresh cilantro plus 4 sprigs, for garnish

- 1 tablespoon white peppercorns, cracked

- 1 pound salmon fillet, skin on

- 4 cups loosely packed baby mesclun or other baby greens mixture

- 1 red bell pepper, cut into julienne

- 1 large Japanese cucumber, thinly sliced

- 2 yellow vine-ripened tomatoes, thinly sliced

To make the vinaigrette, in a bowl, combine the yuzu juice, sugar, and vinegar. Mix well. Slowly whisk in the oil until the mixture thickens. Season with salt and pepper. Chill.

In a mixing bowl, combine the sake, sugar, salt, bay leaf, cilantro, and peppercorns. Place the salmon skin-side down on a large piece of plastic wrap. Cover with the sake mixture and seal with the plastic wrap. Refrigerate for at least 24 hours but not more than 48 hours. (The salmon will get too salty if cured for more than 2 days.) Rinse the salmon with cold water and dry carefully with a dish towel.

Preheat the oven to 200°. Remove the skin from the salmon. (Be sure to remove all the flesh from the skin, or it won't get crisp when cooked.) Place the salmon skin on a baking sheet and bake for 45 minutes, or until the skin is very crisp but not burned. Remove from the oven and let cool slightly. Meanwhile, slice the salmon fillet into very thin slices, about 1/16 inch thick. Chill slightly before using.

Coarsely chop the salmon skin. Transfer to a mixing bowl and combine with the greens and bell pepper. Toss lightly with the vinaigrette.

To assemble, in the center of each of 4 plates, alternate the cucumber and tomato slices, overlapping slightly, to form a circle. Divide the salad evenly among the plates and place on top of the cucumbers and tomatoes. Add the salmon slices around the salad to resemble a pinwheel. Top each with a cilantro sprig.

Miso Chicken

Serves 4

Teriyaki chicken, miso chicken, chicken thighs—these are all staples of "local" Japanese cooking. We call the sauce for this dish "Japanese barbecue sauce." Hopefully, one day we can bottle it. To me, this dish with rice and some Japanese pickles defines perfection.

2 1/2 pounds boneless chicken thighs

2 cups Miso Marinade (page 96)

2 cups shredded napa cabbage

1/2 cup Su-Miso Sauce (page 88)

2 tablespoons finely chopped green onion, green part only, for garnish

1 tablespoon white sesame seeds, for garnish

Place the chicken thighs in a shallow dish and pour the marinade over them. Turn the chicken to coat well, cover, and refrigerate for at least 12 hours.

Prepare a fire in a charcoal grill or preheat a gas grill. Place the chicken on the grill rack. Grill, turning once, 4 to 5 minutes per side, until the juices run clear. Remove from the grill and slice into strips. To serve, divide the cabbage evenly among 4 plates. Top with the chicken strips. Drizzle the sauce over all and top with the green onion and sesame seeds.

Quick-Braised Chicken Livers with Shiitake Mushroom Chips and Rich Wild Mushroom Essence

Serves 4

You don't see many recipes with chicken livers these days. And Tom loves chicken livers because they evoke great childhood memories for him. Here's a dish that's very inexpensive to make and is absolutely delicious.

SHIITAKE MUSHROOM CHIPS

Cottonseed, peanut, or canola oil for deep-frying

2 cups sliced fresh shiitake mushrooms

Kosher salt and freshly ground black pepper

1 1/2 pounds chicken livers

Kosher salt and freshly ground black pepper

1/4 cup all-purpose flour

2 tablespoons cottonseed, peanut, or canola oil

1 teaspoon minced garlic

1/2 cup sliced fresh shiitake mushrooms

2 cups beef broth

1 cup unsalted butter, at room temperature

To make the mushroom chips, in a wok or heavy, deep skillet, pour in the oil to a depth of about 4 inches and heat to 350°. Add the mushrooms and fry for 4 to 5 minutes, until browned. Using a slotted spoon, transfer to paper towels to drain. Season with salt and pepper. Set aside. The chips will get crisp as they cool.

Clean the chicken livers by separating the lobes into individual pieces and removing the fat. Season with salt and pepper. Toss in the flour to coat evenly, shaking off the excess. In a large skillet, heat the oil over medium heat. Add the livers and sauté until crisp, about 5 minutes. Using a slotted spoon, transfer to paper towels to drain. Drain most of the oil from the skillet. Add the garlic and mushrooms and sauté over medium-high heat until the mushrooms are soft, about 3 minutes. Add the broth, decrease the heat to medium, and simmer for 5 minutes.

To serve, arrange the livers and sautéed mushrooms on a serving dish. Add the butter to the skillet, scraping up the browned bits, and whisk until smooth. Pour the browned butter over the livers and mushrooms. Scatter the mushroom chips on top. Serve immediately.

Chinese Five-Spice Duck Salad with Black Plums, Kula Grape Tomatoes, and Roasted Ka'u Orange Vinaigrette

Serves 4

At its heart, this is a traditional duck salad. The flavor and texture of the duck itself is just like the traditional kind of five-spice duck with plum sauce you find in Chinese restaurants all over the country. Since Keith is from the Big Island of Hawai'i, he naturally loves Ka'u oranges, and roasting them really brings out their flavor. For those of you who don't have access to Ka'u oranges, navel oranges are fine. Chinese five-spice powder is available in Asian markets.

ROASTED KA'U ORANGE VINAIGRETTE

1 Ka'u or navel orange

¹/₂ tablespoon canola oil

¹/₄ cup rice vinegar

¹/₂ tablespoon sugar

Pinch of minced garlic

Pinch of peeled and minced fresh ginger

¹/₄ cup extra virgin olive oil

Kosher salt and freshly ground black pepper

1 (8-ounce) Muscovy duck breast, skin on

Kosher salt and freshly ground black pepper

1 teaspoon Chinese five-spice powder

2 teaspoons canola oil

¹/₄ cup chopped macadamia nuts

1 tablespoon macadamia nut oil

12 ounces mixed baby greens

1 cup thinly sliced black plums

1 cup halved vine-ripened grape tomatoes

2 tablespoons micro greens

To make the vinaigrette, preheat the oven to 375°. Rub the orange with the canola oil. Place on a baking sheet and roast for 10 to 12 minutes, or until the orange is very soft and slightly brown. Allow to cool, then juice the orange. In a bowl, whisk the vinegar, sugar, garlic, ginger, and orange juice. Slowly whisk in the olive oil until the mixture is thickened. Season with salt and pepper. Chill. The vinaigrette can be made up to 5 days in advance and can be stored, covered, in the refrigerator.

Season the duck with salt, pepper, and the Chinese five-spice powder. In a sauté pan, heat the oil over medium heat. Add the duck breast, skin-side down, and cook for about 6 minutes per side or until the skin is crisp and the meat is medium-rare. Remove from the heat and let cool slightly, then cut into ¼-inch-thick slices.

Preheat the oven to 375°. In a small bowl, toss the nuts with the nut oil and season with salt and pepper. Transfer to a baking sheet and roast for about 3 minutes, or until golden brown. Let cool.

In a bowl, toss the baby greens, plums, tomatoes, and nuts with the vinaigrette. To serve, divide the salad evenly and place in the center of each of 4 plates. Divide the duck slices and arrange in a pinwheel around each salad. Top each with a few micro greens.

Tea Duck Egg Roll

Created by one of our former chefs, this dish has been on our menu since we opened. So I guess that makes it a sentimental favorite. Bottled hoisin sauce and plum sauce are available in Asian markets.

1 tablespoon cottonseed, peanut, or canola oil

1 cup julienned carrot

1 cup diced Maui onion or other sweet onion

1 tablespoon peeled and minced fresh ginger

1 tablespoon minced garlic

1/2 cup chopped red bell pepper

1 3/4 cups chopped mushrooms (any kind)

1 1/2 cups finely chopped green onion, green part only

4 cups chopped napa cabbage

2 pounds cooked duck meat, shredded

1/4 cup shoyu (Japanese soy sauce)

1/4 cup hoisin sauce

2 teaspoons chopped fresh cilantro

6 (6 by 6-inch) egg roll wrappers

1 egg, slightly beaten

Cottonseed, peanut, or canola oil for deep-frying

Chinese prepared hot mustard, for dipping

Plum sauce, for dipping

Kochujang Dressing (page 109) or sweet Thai chili sauce, for dipping

In a large braising pan, heat the 1 tablespoon oil over medium heat. Add the carrot, onion, ginger, and garlic and sauté for 2 to 3 minutes, or until tender. Add the bell pepper, mushrooms, green onion, and cabbage and continue cooking for about 6 minutes, or until the vegetables have started to wilt. Add the duck meat and mix well. Add the shoyu, hoisin sauce, and cilantro. Decrease the heat to low and cook for 15 minutes, until all the flavors have blended and the mixture is well combined. Remove from the heat and drain. Let cool.

On a clean, dry surface, place the egg roll wrappers. Place one-sixth of the filling in the center of each wrapper. Fold the bottom corner up to cover the filling. Fold the side corners into the center. Brush the edges with egg wash and roll to seal. Repeat with the remaining wrappers and filling to make a total of 6 egg rolls.

In a heavy saucepan, pour in the oil to a depth of about 4 inches and heat to 360°. Add the egg rolls and fry, turning with tongs to cook evenly, until golden brown, about 7 minutes. Using a slotted spoon, transfer to paper towels to drain. Transfer to a platter and serve with prepared Chinese hot mustard, plum sauce, and kochujang dressing on the side.

Duck and Scallion Crepe with Duck Confit, Baby Bok Choy, and Hoisin Vinaigrette

Serves 6

This is a modern twist on a traditional Chinese dish. It's actually a Chinese-style wrap almost exactly like a duck-stuffed bao or bun on which you'd add a little hoisin.

HOISIN VINAIGRETTE

- 2 tablespoons hoisin sauce
- 1/2 cup rice vinegar
- 1/2 tablespoon mirin (sweet rice wine)
- 1 tablespoon shoyu (Japanese soy sauce)
- 1 tablespoon chopped garlic
- 1 tablespoon peeled and chopped fresh ginger
- 1/2 tablespoon Asian (toasted) sesame oil
- 2 cups cottonseed, peanut, or canola oil

- 2 pounds duck legs
- 1/2 tablespoon kosher salt
- 1 teaspoon freshly ground white pepper
- 1/2 tablespoon Chinese five-spice powder

SCALLION CREPES

- 1/2 cup all-purpose flour
- 1/4 teaspoon sugar
- 1/4 teaspoon kosher salt
- 1 egg
- 3/4 cup plus 2 tablespoons milk
- 1/4 cup chopped scallions
- 1/2 cup unsalted butter

- 1 cup baby bok choy, halved lengthwise and cut into 1/2-inch pieces
- 1/4 cup finely chopped green onion, green part only, for garnish
- 1/4 cup kaiware sprouts, for garnish
- 6 fresh cilantro sprigs, for garnish

To prepare the vinaigrette, in a stainless steel bowl, combine the hoisin sauce, vinegar, mirin, shoyu, garlic, and ginger. Slowly whisk in the sesame oil and cottonseed oil until thickened. Chill. The vinaigrette can be made ahead of time and stored in an airtight container in the refrigerator for up to 1 month.

Preheat the oven to 300°. Season the duck with the salt, pepper, and five-spice powder. Transfer the duck to a roasting pan and roast for about 2 hours, turning every 30 minutes, until the meat falls off the bone. Remove from the oven and let stand until cool enough to handle, then shred the meat.

To prepare the crepes, in a food processer, combine the flour, sugar, salt, egg, and milk. Process for 4 minutes, until smooth and thoroughly combined. Transfer the mixture into a bowl and stir in the scallions. Cover and refrigerate for at least 1 hour. Meanwhile, in a small saucepan, slowly melt the butter over very low heat until it begins to separate, about 10 minutes. Remove from the heat. Ladle the clear liquid at the top (about ⅓ cup) and transfer into a container; this is called clarified butter. Set aside until ready to use, and store any leftover amount in the refrigerator, covered. The separated milk solids can be used as buttermilk in other recipes or discarded.

In a 6-inch nonstick sauté pan, heat 1 teaspoon of the clarified butter over medium heat. Spoon in about 2 tablespoons of batter or just enough to coat the bottom of the pan. Swirl the batter in the pan so the batter forms a thin sheet. Cook for about 1 minute on one side and 30 seconds on the other, or until both sides are golden brown. Transfer to paper towels. Repeat with the remaining batter, adding more butter to the pan after every second or third crepe. You should have about 12 crepes in all. Set aside 6 crepes to use for now; the remaining crepes can wrapped and frozen for later use.

In a large stockpot, bring 1 gallon of salted water to a boil over high heat. Add the bok choy and cook for 3 minutes, until tender. Transfer the bok choy to ice water to stop the cooking process and to help retain the color.

If necessary, rewarm the crepes by wrapping them in a damp paper towel and heating them in the microwave on high for 30 seconds. To assemble, place 1 crepe on a cutting board and fill with one-sixth of the duck meat. Place one-sixth of the baby bok choy on top of the duck meat and roll the crepe into a cylinder. Repeat to make a total of 6 crepes. Arrange a rolled crepe in the center of each of 6 plates. Drizzle the hoisin vinaigrette on top and garnish with the green onion, sprouts, and a cilantro sprig in the center of each crepe.

Crystallized Baby Back Ribs with Foie Gras Macaroni and Cheese

Serves 4

Necessity is the mother of invention. When the organizers of an outdoor culinary event ran out of cooking fuel, Tom remembered he had his tools in the back of my truck—including a propane soldering torch. He heated up his already roasted ribs with the torch and used it to caramelize the sugar—kind of like "Baby Back Rib Crème Brûlée." They taste way better than that sounds. And they go best with this very upscale mac & cheese.

RIB MARINADE

- 1/2 cup chili powder
- 1 tablespoon minced garlic
- 1/2 teaspoon chopped fresh thyme
- 1 whole star anise
- 1 (1/2 by 2-inch) slice peeled fresh ginger
- 2 cups shoyu (Japanese soy sauce)
- 1 cup balsamic vinegar
- 1 cup olive oil
- 1 cup vegetable oil

HONEY MUSTARD SAUCE

- 1/4 cup Dijon mustard
- 1 tablespoon honey
- 1 tablespoon red wine vinegar
- 1/2 cup packed brown sugar

- 2 racks baby back ribs

FOIE GRAS MACARONI AND CHEESE

- 3 ounces grade A foie gras, deveined
- Kosher salt and freshly ground black pepper
- 1 1/2 cups cooked macaroni (any shape)
- 1/4 cup cream cheese, at room temperature
- 1/4 cup shredded sharp Cheddar cheese
- 1/4 pound triple-cream Brie, cubed
- 1/2 cup heavy cream
- 1/2 cup Honey Mustard Sauce (above)
- 1/2 cup sugar

(continued)

continued from page 154

To prepare the marinade, in a large bowl, combine the chili powder, garlic, thyme, star anise, ginger, shoyu, and vinegar. Slowly whisk in the olive oil and vegetable oil until the mixture is thickened. The marinade can be made ahead of time and stored in an airtight container in the refigerator for 1 month.

To prepare the sauce, in a bowl, combine the mustard and honey. Add the vinegar and sugar, mixing until smooth. The sauce can be made ahead of time and stored in an airtight container in the refrigerator for 1 month.

Place the ribs in a shallow dish and pour the marinade over them. Turn the ribs to coat well, cover, and refrigerate overnight.

Preheat the oven to 400°. Transfer the ribs to a roasting pan. Bake, covered, for 1 to 1½ hours, or until the meat starts to fall off the bone.

Meanwhile, prepare the macaroni and cheese: Season the foie gras with salt and pepper. In a large skillet, add the foie gras and sear over medium-high heat until brown and caramelized, about 4 minutes. Transfer the foie gras to a strainer and strain the fat into a bowl. Cut the foie gras into a large dice and set aside. In a large bowl, carefully combine the macaroni with all the cheeses until it is completely coated. Season with salt and pepper. In a bowl, combine the foie gras and the cream, then add to the macaroni mixture. Transfer the mixture to a greased casserole dish and place in the oven, either on the same rack as the ribs if it will fit or on another rack. Bake for 25 to 30 minutes, until all the cheeses have melted and the cream has started to reduce and get "gooey." To serve in neat squares, immediately after cooking, chill for 30 minutes, cut into squares, and reheat in the microwave for 1 minute.

Remove the ribs from the oven and brush with the honey mustard sauce. Sprinkle the sugar over all and carefully wave a lit butane torch over the ribs to caramelize the sugar. Alternatively, slip the roasting pan under a hot broiler just long enough to caramelize the sugar, about 5 minutes. Watch closely, as the sugar burns easily. Remove from the broiler and cut into individual ribs.

To serve, spoon a portion of the macaroni and cheese onto the center of each of 4 plates. Top each with 6 ribs stacked on top of each other in a crisscross pattern.

Ginger Fried Ham Hocks with Sweet Pork Broth and Mochi Dumplings

Serves 4

Nothin' Southern about this boy! To Tom's taste, the less expensive and often scorned cuts of pork tend to be the most flavorful. This dish is a play on texture and flavor and exhibits the real properties of New American cuisine: a true fusion of styles and flavors. At its most basic, this recipe is a variation on chicken and dumplings, using pork instead of chicken and sweet rice flour (mochiko) instead of wheat flour. "Ham hock" usually refers to a smoked shin part of the leg, but in our recipe we use an unsmoked shin; you may need to special order it from your butcher. Mochiko, by the way, can be found at Asian markets.

1 tablespoon peeled and chopped fresh ginger

1 tablespoon minced garlic

1 teaspoon chili flakes

1 teaspoon Asian (toasted) sesame oil

1/2 cup olive oil

4 (2-inch-long) pieces fresh, bone-in pork shank

3 cups all-purpose flour

1 tablespoon canola oil

4 cups pork broth or chicken broth

1/4 cup sweet Thai chili sauce

MOCHI DUMPLINGS

2 eggs

1/2 cup half-and-half

1/2 cup all-purpose flour

1/2 cup mochiko (sweet rice flour)

1 teaspoon baking powder

1 serrano chile, seeded and diced

1/2 cup chopped fresh cilantro

1/2 teaspoon kosher salt

Cottonseed, peanut, or canola oil for deep-frying

4 cups mochiko (sweet rice flour)

4 fresh parsley sprigs

(continued)

continued from page 157

In a large stainless steel bowl, combine the ginger, garlic, chili flakes, sesame oil, and olive oil. Add the pork, cover, and marinate for at least 4 hours or overnight in the refrigerator.

Preheat the oven to 350°. Remove the pork from the marinade and roll each piece in the flour to coat evenly, shaking off the excess. In a large skillet, heat the canola oil over medium heat. Add the pork and sear for about 4 minutes per side, until browned.

Transfer the pork to a baking pan and add the broth and chili sauce. Place in the oven and bake, covered, for 45 minutes, or until the meat is just tender. Remove the pork from the pan, pat dry with a towel, and set aside. Reserve the broth from the pan.

To make the mochi dumplings, in a bowl, beat the eggs with the half-and-half until well blended. Add the flour, mochiko, and baking powder and mix until combined. Fold in the chile, cilantro, and salt. The mixture should have the consistency of a thick cake batter. Add the reserved broth to a large saucepan and bring to a simmer over medium-low heat. Drop a heaping tablespoon of the batter into the broth, as many as will fit in the pan without over-lapping, and cook for 10 to 15 minutes, until the dumplings float to the top. Using a slotted spoon, transfer to paper towels to drain. Repeat with remaining batter to make about 8 dumplings. Set aside. Reserve the broth used to cook the dumplings.

In a wok or heavy, deep skillet, pour in the oil to a depth of 4 inches and heat to 350°. Roll the pork in the mochiko to coat evenly. Add the pork to the skillet and fry, turning with tongs to cook evenly, until crisp, about 5 minutes. Using a slotted spoon, transfer to paper towels to drain.

To serve, place 2 dumplings and 1 ham hock in each of 4 large bowls. Spoon ½ cup broth in each bowl. Top each with a parsley sprig.

Seared Buffalo Strip Loin Sashimi with Wasabi Oil, Kim Chee, and Shrimp Chips

Serves 4

Several years ago, the National Bison Association contacted Tom to come up with some dishes for them using, obviously, American buffalo. This is the 2002 recipe. Combine tried-and-true culinary techniques such as the salting (or koshering) of meat with a contemporary use of a classic meat product and local Hawai'i ingredients . . . and there you have it. The shrimp chips are dried shrimp that have been ground and mixed with seasonings. They are packaged similar to potato chips and can be found in Asian markets. You'll need to special-order the buffalo from your butcher or specialty meat market, but it'll be worth it—the meat is delicious, high in protein, and low in fat and cholesterol. The trick is to not over-cook it, or it becomes tough and chewy.

2 pounds whole buffalo strip loin	3 cups kimchee (Korean pickled cabbage)
2 cups kosher salt	
1/4 cup shichimi (seven-spice pepper) or any blackening spice	4 shrimp chips
	1/4 cup wasabi oil
2 tablespoons olive oil	1/4 cup shoyu (Japanese soy sauce)

In a large casserole, place the strip loin and coat with the salt. Cover and refrigerate overnight. Rinse the loin with cold water and cut into 2 by 2-inch cubes. Season with the shichimi. In a skillet, heat the oil over medium-high heat. Add the strip loin and and sear on all sides for 3 to 4 minutes per side, until browned. Remove from the heat and let cool slightly, then cut into 1/4-inch-thick slices.

To serve, divide the slices among 4 plates, arranging them in a fan pattern. Divide the kimchee and place alongside the slices with 1 shrimp chip. Drizzle the wasabi oil and shoyu on top and serve.

Goat Cheese and Wild Mushroom Ravioli with Balsamic Syrup and Sweet Shoyu

Serves 4 to 6

The earthiness of the wild mushrooms and the tartness of the goat cheese are a perfect culinary match. Combining them with the richness and "oaky" quality of the aged balsamic vinegar and the depth of the sweet shoyu makes for pure delight. For the mushrooms in this recipe, use shiitake, oyster, or any wild mushroom that you can find in your local market.

1 tablespoon extra virgin olive oil	Kosher salt and freshly ground black pepper
1/4 cup diced Maui onion or other sweet onion	1 egg
1 teaspoon minced garlic	12 (2 by 2-inch) wonton wrappers or gyoza wrappers
1 1/2 cups wild mushroom, such as shiitake or oyster	2 tablespoons olive oil
1/2 teaspoon fresh thyme leaf	1/4 cup balsamic vinegar
1/4 cup goat cheese	1/2 cup sweet shoyu (kecap manis)

In a skillet, heat the 1 tablespoon extra virgin olive oil over medium heat. Add the onion and garlic and sauté for 3 to 4 minutes, until translucent. Add the mushrooms and thyme and cook for 4 minutes, or until the mushrooms are tender. Remove from the heat and let cool.

Crumble the goat cheese into a large bowl and add the mushroom mixture. Season with salt and pepper. In a small bowl, whisk together the egg and 1 tablespoon of water to make an egg wash. On a clean, dry surface, lay the wonton wrappers. Fill each one with 2 1/2 teaspoons of the mushroom and goat cheese mixture. Brush the edges with egg wash and fold the wrapper, corner to corner, over the filling, forming a triangle. Press around the filling, forcing any excess air out, and seal the ravioli. Chill for 30 minutes.

Fill a large saucepan with 2 quarts of water, add the 2 tablespoons olive oil, and bring to a boil. Decrease the heat to medium, add the ravioli, and poach for about 5 minutes, or until tender; drain. To serve, place 2 to 3 ravioli on each plate. Drizzle with the balsamic vinegar and sweet shoyu.

Restaurant Row Escargot

Serves 4

Our updated take on classic escargot. I really love it . . . and can never figure out why more people don't order it!

1/2 cup pancetta

1/4 cup diced Maui onion or other sweet onion

1 tablespoon minced garlic

2 cups packed baby spinach

24 medium canned escargot, washed and rinsed

Kosher salt and freshly ground black pepper

1/3 cup Ginger-Lime-Chili Butter Sauce (page 85)

12 (3-inch) baguette slices, toasted

1 tablespoon chopped fresh chives, for garnish

In a medium sauté pan, add the pancetta and cook over medium heat for about 2 minutes, until browned. Add the onion and garlic and cook for about 2 minutes, until translucent. Add the spinach and escargot, mixing well. Season with salt and pepper. Add the sauce and toss to coat well.

To serve, place the baguette slices on a platter and pour the escargot mixture on top. Sprinkle the chives over all and serve immediately.

Crispy Unagi and Foie Gras Napoleon

Serves 4

Ivan has loved unagi since he was a kid. When he grew up and discovered foie gras, he thought the two ingredients would be very complementary to each other. This dish makes people smile. Everybody loves crispy; everybody loves crunchy.

1 cup all-purpose flour

1 cup tempura batter mix

4 (2-ounce) pieces prepared fresh-water eel (unagi)

2 cups panko (Japanese breadcrumbs)

2 tablespoons cooked blue crabmeat

1 teaspoon mayonnaise

2 cups Sushi Rice (page 76)

1 tablespoon julienned gari (pickled ginger)

1 tablespoon finely chopped green onion, green part only

Cottonseed, peanut, or canola oil for deep-frying

8 ounces foie gras, deveined and sliced into 4 pieces

$^1/_4$ cup Unagi Sauce (page 89)

In a large bowl, combine the flour, tempura batter mix, and 1 cup water and stir until it is the consistency of a lumpy pancake batter. Dip the unagi in the batter to coat completely, then firmly press the panko onto each piece. Thread a 6-inch bamboo skewer through each unagi piece to resemble a lollipop, making a total of 4 skewers. Chill for 15 minutes.

Meanwhile, in a small bowl, combine the crabmeat and mayonnaise and mix thoroughly. In another bowl, combine the rice, gari, and green onion. Add the crab mixture and mix thoroughly. Using your hands, mold the mixture into 4 rectangular rice balls, about the size used for nigiri sushi.

In a wok or heavy, deep skillet, pour in the oil to a depth of 3 inches and heat to 350°. Add the unagi skewers to the oil and fry for about 3 minutes, or until golden brown.

In a sauté pan, add the foie gras and sear over medium-high heat for about 2 minutes per side, until medium-rare and nicely browned.

To serve, place 1 rice ball in the center of each of 4 plates. Lean 1 unagi against the side of the rice, at an angle with the skewer pointing up. Lay the foie gras on the unagi and drizzle the unagi sauce over all.

Smoked Japanese Eggplant and Shredded Duck Consommé

Serves 4

This recipe is not for the faint of heart. Even for a professional, making a consommé is a very time-consuming and labor-intensive operation. But the outcome in terms of clarity of appearance and brightness of flavor makes this a diamond of a dish. The smoked and dried eggplants are also important components, but if that proves to be too difficult, then using roasted eggplant for the puree and grilled eggplant slices for the topping are acceptable substitutes.

12 Japanese eggplants, halved lengthwise

1/4 cup kosher salt

1 (4- to 5-pound) whole duck

1/2 cup plus 2 tablespoons canola oil

1 onion, chopped

3 stalks celery, chopped

1 carrot, chopped

2 bay leaves

6 whole peppercorns

1 whole star anise

1 head garlic, halved

1/2 pound ground pork

4 egg whites

Pinch of kosher salt

Pinch of freshly ground black pepper

Place the eggplant on a wire rack and cover with the salt. Place the rack on a large plate to catch the drips and refrigerate overnight. Rinse the eggplant thoroughly and quickly pat dry.

Prepare a smoker and smoke the eggplant for 12 minutes. Or, make your own smoker: In a bowl, place 1/2 cup of wood chips, adding water to cover. Let stand for 15 minutes, then drain. Find a large covered pot that you don't mind getting messy. Place the wood chips in the bottom of that pot and set over high heat. Lay a piece of aluminum foil on top of the chips and place the eggplant on the foil. Cover the pot. As soon as smoke begins to emerge from the pot, remove from the heat. Leave the eggplant in the pot for 12 minutes, then

(continued)

continued from page 163

carefully remove from the heat. Reserve 4 of the eggplant slices. In a food processor, puree the remaining eggplant. Place the reserved eggplant on a wire rack and dry for 12 hours in a 150° oven. Cut each slice in half to make a total of 8 pieces. Cover and set aside at room temperature until ready to use.

To prepare the stock for the consommé, cut up the duck, removing the bones; set aside the meat. In a large saucepan, heat ½ cup of the canola oil over medium-high heat. Add the bones and the neck and cook for 15 minutes, until browned. Transfer the bones and neck to a 5-quart stockpot. Add the onion, celery, carrot, bay leaves, peppercorns, star anise, and garlic. Cover with water, set over high heat, and bring to a boil. Reduce the heat to medium and simmer, uncovered, for 3 hours, skimming off the fat and impurities as needed (reserve the skimmed fat and store, covered, in the refrigerator, to use later). Remove from the heat and strain the liquid through a fine-mesh sieve. Cover and refrigerate overnight (the stock can be divided into several smaller containers).

Preheat the oven to 400°. Using a spoon, remove the layer of fat from the top of the stock and add it to the skimmed fat that was reserved earlier; set aside. Transfer the stock back to the 5-quart stockpot. In a bowl, mix together the ground pork, eggplant puree, egg whites, salt, and pepper. Transfer the pork mixture to the stockpot with the duck stock and bring to a simmer over low heat. The pork will form a "raft" floating on the stock. Do not stir. Cook for 15 minutes. Break a hole in the edge of the pork "raft" and start to remove it and the impurities from the stock. The consommé will be a rich golden color. After all the impurities and the pork have been removed, strain the consommé through an extremely fine-mesh sieve. Keep chilled until ready to use.

To prepare the duck meat, in a large skillet, heat the remaining 2 tablespoons canola oil over medium heat and sear the duck breast and leg meat until golden brown, about 4 minutes per side. Transfer the duck meat to a casserole dish and cover with the skimmed duck fat and oil from the stockpot. Cover the casserole dish with aluminum foil and bake for 2 hours. Remove from the oven and let cool. Remove the fat from the duck meat and shred the meat with a fork. Set aside.

Just before serving, return the consommé to a large saucepan and reheat over medium heat. To serve, ladle the consommé into 4 bowls. Divide the duck meat among the bowls and top with 2 pieces each of the reserved eggplant.

Wok-Fried Baby Leeks with Spicy Sausage and Upcountry Vegetables

Serves 4

Tom created this recipe from the leftovers of an all-vegetarian meal. For his own personal enjoyment, he added the spicy sausage! Infusing oil with flavors is very easy. Just add the herb or other flavor to the oil and set aside in an airtight jar. The longer you leave it, the more infused and flavorful the oil gets. You can serve this dish over torn pasta or pappardelle; it's also great with rice.

1 tablespoon vegetable oil

1 pound hot Italian sausage, cut into 1-inch cubes

1 1/2 tablespoons chili oil, infused with a slice of ginger

1 teaspoon peeled and minced fresh ginger

1 1/2 cups assorted diced vegetables (squash, broccoli, mushrooms, carrots, etc.)

12 baby leeks, bottoms trimmed

1/2 cup chicken stock

1/2 cup fresh pineapple sage, hand torn, or 1 tablespoon fresh sage, hand torn

1/2 tablespoon white miso (soybean paste)

2 tablespoons unsalted butter, at room temperature

In a wok or heavy, deep skillet, heat the oil over medium-high heat. Add the sausage and cook until browned, about 8 minutes. Remove the sausage and set aside. Discard the oil and wipe the wok clean to use again.

In the same wok, add the chili oil, ginger, and vegetables and heat over medium-high heat for about 3 minutes, until the vegetables are tender. Remove from the heat and drain, reserving a quarter of the liquid in a saucepan. Set aside the vegetables. Add the leeks and stock to the reserved liquid and cook over medium heat for about 5 minutes, until the leeks are tender. Set aside the leeks and add the stock to the wok along with the vegetables and sausage and sauté over high heat until heated through, about 5 minutes. Add the pineapple sage and miso, stirring to dissolve the miso. Add the butter, stirring to combine.

To serve, divide the leeks among 4 plates and spoon the sausage mixture on top of each.

Keahole Lobster Ramen with Lobster and Tarragon Butter Croutons

Serves 4

The Maine lobsters grown in Keahole on the island of Hawai'i are known for their sweet flavor. The fact that they're local means we can get them regularly and fresh from the tanks. This dish takes a simple, home-style, comfort dish and elevates it to a gourmet level, combining classical and Asian flavors and techniques. Of course, if you don't live in Hawai'i, you won't be able to get Keahole lobster meat, so instead buy the freshest lobster you can find. You can also try this recipe with any other shellfish. Just be sure you get the freshest available. Lobster tomalley is a creamy green substance that can be easily scooped out from the lobster body.

LOBSTER AND TARRAGON BUTTER CROUTONS

- 1 teaspoon chopped fresh tarragon
- 1/2 teaspoon lobster tomalley (liver)
- 1/4 cup unsalted butter, at room temperature
- 1 tablespoon plain breadcrumbs or panko (Japanese breadcrumbs)
- 1 teaspoon chopped fresh chives
- Kosher salt and freshly ground black pepper
- 8 (3/4-inch) slices sourdough bread

- 8 cups Lobster Stock (page 94)
- 1 pound Maine lobster meat
- 1/2 cup low-sodium shoyu (Japanese soy sauce)
- 1 tablespoon hondashi (Japanese soup base)
- 1 cup sake
- 1 pound fresh ramen noodles
- 1/4 teaspoon peeled and grated fresh ginger
- 2 tablespoons finely chopped green onion, green part only
- 2 tablespoons unsalted butter, at room temperature
- 4 sprigs fresh tarragon, for garnish
- 4 lime wedges, for garnish

To make the croutons, preheat the oven to 350°. In a bowl, fold the tarragon and lobster tomalley into the butter. Stir in the breadcrumbs and chives and season with salt and pepper. Spread the butter mixture on the bread slices and transfer to a baking sheet. Bake on the middle rack of the oven for about 5 minutes, or until golden brown. Set aside.

In a large saucepan, add the stock and heat over high heat. Add the lobster meat and poach for 3 minutes, until the meat is white. Using a fine-mesh sieve or slotted spoon, transfer the lobster meat to a container and keep in the refrigerator until ready to use. Add the shoyu to the stock and bring to a simmer over medium heat. Add the hondashi. In a small saucepan, heat the sake over medium-high heat to cook off the alcohol, about 5 minutes, and add to the stock. Simmer over medium heat for 10 minutes, skimming off any impurities as necessary.

Meanwhile, bring a large saucepan filled with water to a boil. Add the noodles and cook for 5 minutes, until tender; drain. Add the noodles to the stock. Slice the lobster meat into medallions. Add the lobster meat, ginger, and green onion to the stock. Add the butter, stirring to combine.

To serve, divide the noodles, lobster, and broth among 4 bowls. Top with the croutons. Garnish each bowl with a sprig of tarragon and a lime wedge.

Ramen with Foie Gras

Every kid in Hawai'i eats ramen—some eat it every day. It's basically Japanese noodles. I haven't seen gourmet ramen, just traditional, so we experimented and came up with this recipe. It has a nice, rich broth. Here's an upscale ramen that I've never seen anywhere else.

1 (2-inch-square) piece konbu (kelp)

2 cups katsuobushi (bonito flakes)

$1/2$ cup shoyu (Japanese soy sauce)

1 tablespoon hondashi (Japanese soup base)

4 cups fresh ramen noodles

1 cup julienned carrot

8 ounces foie gras, deveined and sliced into 4 pieces

4 teaspoons finely chopped green onion, green part only

Kosher salt and freshly ground black pepper

To prepare the broth, in a large saucepan, heat 8 cups of water over high heat. Add the konbu, katsuobushi, and shoyu and bring almost to a boil. Remove from the heat and, using a fine-mesh sieve, strain the liquid. Stir in the hondashi. Set aside and keep warm.

Fill another large saucepan with water and bring to a boil. Add the noodles and cook for 5 minutes, until tender; drain.

To serve, divide the noodles among 4 bowls. Top each with the carrot and 1 piece of foie gras. Pour the hot broth over the foie gras, garnish with the green onion, and season with salt and pepper.

Big Plates

Seared Day Boat Scallops, Okinawan
   Sweet Potatoes, Butter-Braised Leeks,
   and Sweet Unagi Glaze | 173

Chili-Glazed King Crab Legs with Chinese
   Peas and Toasted Almonds | 174

Keahole Lobster and Potato–Goat
   Cheese Galettes with Wasabi Lobster
   Broth | 176

Butter-Braised Kona Maine Lobster,
   Corn Flan, Sweet Corn Sauce, and
   Shaved Black Truffles | 178

Pan-Seared Mahimahi, Butternut Squash
   Ravioli, Sautéed Spinach, and Honey-
   Sesame Butter Sauce | 180

Pan-Braised Mahimahi with Pancetta
   Lardons, Shiso, and Vine-Ripened
   Tomato Vinaigrette | 181

Prosciutto-Wrapped Mahimahi with
   Truffle-Asparagus Cream | 182

Caper-Crusted Opakapaka with Tobiko
   Beurre Blanc | 183

Furikake-Crusted Opakapaka on
   Udon Noodles with Sweet Garlic-
   Lobster Butter | 185

Steamed Opakapaka, Lobster Tortellini,
   Morel Mushroom Broth, and Ma'alaea
   Asparagus | 186

Opakapaka "En Croute," Shiitake Mushroom Duxelle, Baby Bok Choy, and
   Gingered Carrot Emulsion | 188

Crispy-Skin Onaga, Chinese Long Beans,
   Cake Noodle, and Ginger Beurre
   Blanc | 190

Steamed Kahuku Farm-Raised Moi,
   Black Bean Paste, Ong Choy, and
   Shiitake Nage | 193

Pan-Seared Moi with Crispy Oxtail
   Ravioli | 194

Roasted Hawaiian Lehi, Sansei Spicy
   Crab, Roasted Eggplant and Sweet
   Potato Tian, and Sweet Carrot
   Emulsion | 196

Miso-Roasted Hapu'upu'u with Honey-
  Sesame Butter Sauce | 197

Pan-Braised Weke with Anchovy-Tomato
  Sauce | 198

Japanese-Style Jerk Chicken | 199

Miso-Honey-Marinated Duck Breast with
  Black Rice Risotto and Yuzu | 200

Smoked Maple Leaf Duck Breast
  with Japanese Eggplant and
  Plum Wine | 202

Mild Chili and Porcini–Dusted Beef
  Filet, Garlic Mashed Potatoes, and
  Shiitake Mushroom with Unagi
  Demi-Glace | 203

Braised Short Ribs with Spicy Thai Curry
  Sauce | 204

Beef Tenderloin on Udon Noodles with
  Demi-Glace | 206

Gorgonzola-Stuffed Filet, Wild Mushroom Ragout, Maui Onion Demi-
  Glace, and Okinawan Sweet Potato
  Mousse | 207

Seared Day Boat Scallops, Okinawan Sweet Potatoes, Butter-Braised Leeks, and Sweet Unagi Glaze

Serves 4

We made this dish for the grand opening of a Star Market store (a local Hawai'i supermarket chain) in Kailua, O'ahu. One of the items that was accessible to us for the event happened to be day boat scallops. We were very lucky that day. When you can get them, there's nothing better. The leeks, like the scallops, melt in your mouth. And we bring it all home with a little drizzle of sweet unagi glaze.

1 1/2 pounds Okinawan sweet potatoes or yams, peeled and diced

1 teaspoon peeled and minced fresh ginger

1 cup milk

3 tablespoons unsalted butter

1 pound leeks, white part only, cut in half lengthwise

1/4 teaspoon salt

Pinch of freshly ground white pepper

2 cups chicken stock

1 cup heavy cream

8 large day boat or sea scallops

1 tablespoon olive oil

3 tablespoons Unagi Sauce (page 89)

1 tablespoon flying fish roe (tobiko), for garnish

In a large saucepan, bring water to a boil over high heat. Place the potatoes in the water and boil until tender, about 30 minutes. Drain and return to the pot. In a small saucepan, combine the ginger and milk and heat over medium heat until it just comes to a boil, then remove from the heat. Add the milk mixture and 2 tablespoons of the butter to the potatoes. Using a potato masher, mash to a creamy consistency.

In a sauté pan, heat the remaining 1 tablespoon of butter over medium-high heat. Add the leek, salt, and pepper and sauté for 3 to 4 minutes, until tender. Add the chicken stock and cream, decrease the heat to low, and braise the leeks for about 15 minutes, until very soft.

(continued)

continued from page 173

Season the scallops with salt and pepper. In a sauté pan, heat the oil over high heat. Add the scallops and sear for about 2 minutes per side, until they are a light golden brown. Set aside.

To serve, place a mound of the sweet potatoes in the center of each of 4 plates. Top with a quarter of the leek. Top the leeks with 2 scallops each. Drizzle the unagi sauce over the scallops and top with the tobiko.

Chili-Glazed King Crab Legs with Chinese Peas and Toasted Almonds

Serves 4

This is another serve-it-on-a-big-platter, everybody-dig-in, family-style dish. The flavors explode in your mouth. For king crab lovers, this is *da one!*

4 cups sweet Thai chili sauce

2 tablespoons sambal (Indonesian chili paste)

1/4 cup minced garlic

2 tablespoons fish sauce (patis)

1/4 cup rice vinegar

4 pounds king crab legs, split in half lengthwise

2 cups snow peas

1/4 cup chopped fresh cilantro

2 tablespoons finely chopped green onion, green part only

1 cup slivered almonds, toasted

In a hot wok, add the chili sauce, sambal, garlic, fish sauce, and vinegar and simmer for 5 minutes over medium-low heat, until heated through and all the flavors combine. Add the crab and toss to coat completely. Increase the heat to high and cook for 4 minutes, until the crab is cooked and everything is hot. Add the snow peas, cilantro, and green onion and mix well. Cook for 4 minutes, until hot. To serve, transfer the crab, vegetables, and sauce to a large platter and sprinkle the almonds over all.

Keahole Lobster and Potato-Goat Cheese Galettes with Wasabi Lobster Broth

Serves 4

This is a great dish to make for company. It can be set up and prepared the night before or the morning of your party, which allows you to both enjoy your guests and serve an extravagant and delicious dish. Save the scraps; they make great snacks.

WASABI LOBSTER BROTH

3 cups Lobster Stock (page 94) or shellfish stock

1/4 cup sake

1 teaspoon peeled and minced fresh ginger

1/4 cup mirin (sweet rice wine)

1/4 cup wasabi paste

1/2 cup unsalted butter, at room temperature

POTATO-GOAT CHEESE GALETTE

1 teaspoon unsalted butter

1/2 cup sliced Maui onion or other sweet onion

3 medium Yukon Gold potatoes, sliced lengthwise about 1/8-inch thick

1 1/2 cups goat cheese, crumbled

Kosher salt and freshly ground black pepper

1 cup heavy cream

2 (1 1/2-pound) Maine lobsters, poached and halved, meat removed from shells

4 sugarcane sticks, for garnish

1/4 cup sweet shoyu (kecap manis), for garnish

To prepare the broth, in a saucepan, combine the stock, sake, ginger, mirin, and wasabi paste and bring to a boil over high heat. Decrease the heat to medium and simmer for 15 minutes, until all of the flavors combine. Whisk in the butter until mixed completely. Strain the mixture through a fine-mesh sieve, return it to the saucepan, and keep warm until ready to serve. The broth can be stored in an airtight container in the refrigerator for up to 1 week.

To prepare the galette, preheat the oven to 450°. Grease a shallow baking dish or 9-inch pie pan. In a skillet, heat the butter over medium-high heat, add the onion, and sauté until golden brown, about 8 minutes. In the baking dish, layer the potatoes three deep. Top with one-sixth of the goat cheese and onion and season with salt and pepper. Repeat layering the ingredients to make a total of six layers. Pour the cream over all. Bake, covered, for 30 minutes, or until the potatoes are tender. Let stand for 10 minutes before cutting, and cut into any desired shape (for example, circles, diamonds, squares). Galettes can be prepared ahead of time and reheated just before serving for 6 to 7 minutes in a 400° oven, or until just heated through.

To serve, place 1 galette portion on each of 4 plates and top each with the meat from half a lobster tail. Skewer each claw meat with 1 sugar cane and insert in the galette. Pour hot broth around each plate, drizzle the sweet shoyu on top, and serve.

Butter-Braised Kona Maine Lobster, Corn Flan, Sweet Corn Sauce, and Shaved Black Truffles

Serves 4

There's no way to describe this dish but "sweet." The truffles lend earthiness to it. To my palate, there's no better match than corn, lobster, and truffles.

CORN SAUCE

- 3 cups fresh corn kernels, cobs reserved (about 6 ears)
- 2 cups chicken stock
- 2 cups heavy cream
- 1 cup unsalted butter, cold, cut into small pieces
- 2 (10-ounce) Maine lobster tails
- Kosher salt and freshly ground black pepper
- 2 cups unsalted butter

CORN FLAN

- Unsalted butter, for greasing
- 3 cups heavy cream
- 2 cups fresh corn kernels (about 4 ears)
- 3 eggs, beaten
- 1 teaspoon white truffle oil, plus additional for garnish
- 1 teaspoon finely chopped fresh chives
- 1/2 cup micro greens, for garnish
- 1 whole black truffle, shaved, for garnish
- 2 teaspoons flying fish roe (tobiko), for garnish

To prepare the sauce, in a saucepan, combine the corn, cobs, and 1½ cups water. Place the pan over low heat, add the stock and cream, and simmer for about 30 minutes, to allow the flavors to thoroughly combine. Strain through a fine-mesh sieve. Return the mixture to high heat and reduce by a quarter, about 5 minutes. Slowly whisk in the butter. Keep warm until ready to use. The sauce can be stored in an airtight container in the refrigerator for up to 1 week.

To prepare the lobster, cut the lobster tails in half and remove the meat from the shells. Season with salt and pepper. In a sauté pan with a cover, heat the butter over low heat, add the lobster meat, and braise, covered, for 6 to 10 minutes, until just opaque. (It's very important to braise over low heat, so the lobster meat does not overcook.) Let cool, then slice the lobster meat into medallions.

To prepare the flan, preheat the oven to 325°. Grease 4 ovenproof ramekins with the butter. In a saucepan, heat the cream and corn over medium heat, about 10 minutes, then remove from the heat and let stand for 15 minutes, to allow the flavors to combine. In a bowl, slowly whisk 1 cup of the hot cream mixture with the eggs to temper. Tempering will slowly bring the eggs up to the temperature of the cream without scrambling the eggs. Add the egg mixture, truffle oil, and chives to the saucepan with the cream mixture and whisk until smooth. Divide the mixture and pour into the ramekins and place the ramekins in an ovenproof dish or baking pan with high sides. Slide the middle rack partially out of the oven and place the dish on the rack. Pour warm water to a depth of about 1 inch, making sure none of the water comes over the sides and into the dishes. Very carefully slide the rack back into the oven. Bake for 20 minutes or until the custard is set. Carefully remove the ramekins from the water and let cool slightly before handling.

To serve, unmold the flan and place 1 in the center of each of 4 plates. Top each flan with a quarter of the greens. Arrange the lobster medallions in a fan pattern around the flan. Ladle the sauce around the flan. Top each with the truffle shavings, tobiko, and a drizzle of truffle oil.

Pan-Seared MahiMahi, Butternut Squash Ravioli, Sautéed Spinach, and Honey-Sesame Butter Sauce

Serves 4

Mahimahi is probably the most popular local fish for visitors to the Islands. This is a very elegant version of our local mahimahi plate lunch. We dress it up with the ravioli (instead of the usual macaroni salad and two scoops of rice). And instead of soy sauce, a little Honey-Sesame Butter Sauce!

2 cups peeled, seeded, and diced butternut squash

1 tablespoon freshly grated Romano cheese

Kosher salt and freshly ground black pepper

8 (2 by 2-inch) wonton wrappers

4 (4-ounce) mahimahi fillets

1 tablespoon vegetable oil

2 cups spinach, sautéed

1 cup Honey-Sesame Butter Sauce (page 84)

In a large saucepan, boil 4 cups water over high heat. Add the squash and boil for about 20 minutes, until tender. Drain and transfer the squash to a bowl. Add the cheese, mixing well, and season with salt and pepper. On a clean, dry surface, lay the wonton wrappers. Place 1 tablespoon of the squash mixture in the center of each wrapper. Brush the edges with a small amount of water and fold into a triangle, making sure the seal is tight on all sides. Repeat to make a total of 8 ravioli.

Bring a saucepan of salted water to a boil over high heat. Add the ravioli and cook for 3 minutes. Drain and keep warm until ready to serve.

Season the mahimahi with salt and pepper. In a sauté pan, add the vegetable oil and heat over high heat. Add the mahimahi and sear for about 3 minutes per side, until light golden brown on the outside.

To serve, place 2 ravioli in the center of each of 4 plates. Divide the spinach and place on top of the ravioli. Top each with 1 mahimahi. Ladle the sauce around the plate.

Pan-Braised Mahimahi with Pancetta Lardons, Shiso, and Vine-Ripened Tomato Vinaigrette

Serves 4

The pancetta gives this very popular—and quite common—fish a nice smoky flavor. The shiso adds a refreshing finish to the dish.

- 1/2 cup pancetta, cut into 1/2-inch cubes
- 4 (6-ounce) mahimahi fillets
- Kosher salt and freshly ground black pepper
- 1 teaspoon vegetable oil

- 2 cups chicken broth
- 1 cup grape tomatoes, halved
- 1/2 cup unsalted butter
- 4 cups Mashed Potatoes (page 99)
- 3 shiso (perilla) leaves, cut into chiffonade

To prepare the lardons, in a skillet, add the pancetta and sauté over medium heat until crisp, about 5 minutes. Transfer to paper towels to drain and set aside.

To prepare the mahimahi, preheat the oven to 400°. Season the mahimahi with salt and pepper. In a large, ovenproof sauté pan, heat the oil over high heat. Add the mahimahi and sear for about 2 minutes on one side, until lightly browned. Flip over, add three-quarters of the pancetta, and cook for 2 minutes. Add the broth and carefully place the pan in the oven. Bake for 5 minutes, until the flesh is opaque and juicy. Remove the fish from the pan and set aside. Return the pan to high heat and reduce the liquid by half, about 6 minutes. Add the tomatoes and whisk in the butter to make a sauce.

To serve, spoon 1 cup of mashed potatoes onto the center of each of 4 plates. Top each with 1 mahimahi. Ladle the sauce over the fish. Sprinkle the remaining pancetta and the shiso leaves over all.

Prosciutto-Wrapped Mahimahi with Truffle-Asparagus Cream

Serves 4

When Ivan was in New York to cook at the James Beard House in 2000, he tasted a prosciutto-wrapped halibut at a French bistro in the city. He knew it would work well with our local mahimahi and since then has periodically offered this dish as a special at the restaurant.

TRUFFLE-ASPARAGUS CREAM

2 cups dry white wine

2 cups heavy cream

10 spears asparagus, chopped

3 tablespoons Truffle Butter (page 93)

8 tablespoons unsalted butter

Kosher salt and freshly ground white
   pepper

4 (6-ounce) mahimahi fillets

4 thin slices prosciutto

1 tablespoon vegetable oil

4 cups Mashed Potatoes (page 99)

To prepare the cream, in a saucepan, heat the wine over high heat until reduced by half, about 10 minutes. Add the cream and reduce by a quarter, 4 to 5 minutes. Add the asparagus, decrease the heat to medium, and simmer for 2 minutes. Transfer the asparagus mixture to a blender and, with the motor running on medium speed, add the butters, 1 tablespoon at a time, until well blended, about 30 seconds; season with salt and pepper. Set aside and keep warm until ready to serve.

Preheat the oven to 350°. Wrap each mahimahi with 1 slice prosciutto. In a large, oven-proof sauté pan, heat the oil over high heat. Add the fish and lightly sear for about 2 minutes per side, until the prosciutto has browned. Carefully place the pan in the oven and bake for 5 minutes, until the flesh is opaque and juicy.

To serve, place 1 cup of mashed potatoes in the center of each of 4 plates. Top each with 1 mahimahi. Ladle the cream around the fish and serve.

Caper-Crusted Opakapaka with Tobiko Beurre Blanc

Serves 4

A customer came into the Kapalua restaurant one night craving capers. We didn't even have any capers; Ivan had to run over to the Kapalua Bay Hotel to get them. Once he had the capers, he didn't want to do something as simple as a caper butter. So he used them to crust the fresh opakapaka being served that night. And the customer was ecstatic: She wanted the recipe. Here it is. Ivan thinks she only loved him for his capers.

1 cup dry white wine

¹/₂ cup heavy cream

¹/₂ cup unsalted butter

2 tablespoons flying fish roe (tobiko)

Kosher salt and freshly ground black pepper

¹/₂ cup capers, plus additional for garnish

2 egg whites

1 cup panko (Japanese breadcrumbs)

2 tablespoons vegetable oil

4 (6-ounce) opakapaka fillets

To prepare the sauce, in a saucepan, add the wine and cook over high heat until reduced by half, about 4 minutes. Add the cream and cook to reduce by half again, 8 minutes. Carefully whisk in the butter and tobiko. Season with salt and pepper and keep warm.

Preheat the oven to 400°. In a bowl, crush the capers using the back of a spoon. Combine with the egg whites and panko and season with salt and pepper. In a large, ovenproof sauté pan, heat 1 tablespoon of the oil over medium-high heat. Add the opakapaka and lightly sear until rare, about 2 minutes per side. Remove from the pan and let cool for 5 minutes. Wipe the pan to reuse. Using your hands, firmly pat each fillet with the caper mixture to coat on one side only.

In the same pan, heat the remaining 1 tablespoon oil over medium heat, add the opakapaka, coated side down, and cook for about 3 minutes, until light golden brown and crisp. Flip and cook the other side for 3 minutes, until golden brown. Carefully place the sauté pan in the oven and bake for 3 to 5 minutes, until the opakapaka is slightly opaque. (Be careful not to overcook, or the fish will be dry.)

To serve, ladle the sauce onto each of 4 plates, top with the fish, and garnish with the remaining capers.

Furikake-Crusted Opakapaka On Udon Noodles with Sweet Garlic-Lobster Butter

Serves 4

This is so good, the noodles would stand up as a delicious dish all on their own. But it's so much better, of course, with the fish. The furikake seasoning on the fish really makes it special, and the colors and flavors are great.

4 (6-ounce) opakapaka fillets or any snapper

$^1/_4$ cup furikake (rice seasoning)

2 tablespoons peanut oil

$^1/_8$ cup thinly sliced garlic

2 cups Lobster Stock (page 94)

$^1/_2$ cup unsalted butter

Kosher salt and freshly ground black pepper

3 (8-ounce) packages udon noodles, boiled and drained

$^1/_2$ pound fresh spinach

$^1/_2$ cup freshly shredded Parmesan cheese

Turn the opakapaka in the furikake to coat evenly. In a sauté pan, heat 1 tablespoon of the oil over medium-high heat. Add the opakapaka and sear until medium, about 3 minutes on each side. Keep warm until ready to serve.

In a large sauté pan, heat the remaining 1 tablespoon oil over medium-high heat. Add the garlic and sauté until translucent, about 2 minutes. Add the lobster stock and cook until heated through, about 6 minutes. Whisk in the butter until smooth and season with salt and pepper. Add the noodles, spinach, and half of the cheese, tossing to coat.

To serve, divide the noodles and place in the center of each of 4 plates. Top each with 1 opakapaka and sprinkle the remaining cheese over all.

Steamed Opakapaka, Lobster Tortellini, Morel Mushroom Broth, and Ma'alaea Asparagus

Serves 4

Keith loves Italian food. This dish grew out of that love. He thought about making tortellini and adding opakapaka cooked in the best way he knows how: steamed. Morel season—late spring to early summer—is the time to make this dish. We use Ma'alaea asparagus because we support local farmers as much as we possibly can.

1 teaspoon oil

1 teaspoon thinly sliced garlic

2 tablespoons minced onion

1 cup halved fresh morel mushrooms

1 cup trimmed enoki mushrooms

1/2 cup sliced shiitake mushrooms

4 cups chicken stock

1 (8-ounce) lobster tail, meat removed and diced

1 teaspoon chopped fresh tarragon

1 tablespoon chopped bamboo shoots

1 teaspoon finely chopped green onion, green part only

12 (2 by 2-inch) wonton wrappers

1 egg, lightly beaten

4 (4-ounce) opakapaka fillets or any snapper

Kosher salt and freshly ground black pepper

4 ounces asparagus, cut into 1-inch pieces

1/4 cup micro greens, for garnish

To prepare the broth, in a skillet, heat the oil over medium heat. Add the garlic and onion and sauté for 2 minutes, until translucent but making sure they don't brown. Add the mushrooms and cook until tender, about 3 minutes. Add the stock, decrease the heat to low, and cook for 10 minutes, until the liquid is reduced by half and all the flavors have combined. Keep warm until ready to serve.

To prepare the tortellini, in a small bowl, combine the lobster meat, tarragon, bamboo shoots, and green onion. Season with salt and pepper. On a clean, dry surface, lay the wonton wrappers. Place 1½ teaspoons of the lobster mixture in the center of each wrapper. Brush the edges with the egg and fold into a triangle, sealing well on all sides. Set aside.

To prepare the fish, season the opakapaka on both sides with salt and pepper. In a bamboo steamer or on a rack over ½ inch of warm water in a covered pan, add the opakapaka and steam until flaky and cooked through, 5 to 6 minutes. Set aside and keep warm.

Bring a large pot of salted water to a boil. Decrease the heat to medium and gently add the tortellini. Cook for 2 minutes, until tender. Using a slotted spoon, remove the tortellini and set aside; keep the water.

Add the asparagus to the same pot of water and simmer over medium heat for 4 minutes, or until bright green and just a little bit limp.

Just before serving, add the asparagus to the mushroom broth. Place 3 tortellini each in the center of 4 bowls. Top each with 1 opakapaka. Ladle the broth into the bowl. Top with the greens and serve immediately.

Opakapaka "En Croute," Shiitake Mushroom Duxelle, Baby Bok Choy, and Gingered Carrot Emulsion

Serves 4

This is Keith's version of the classic Beef Wellington. Since we live in Hawai'i with an abundance of fresh fish, he naturally substituted a nice moist, flaky, mild white fish. He actually made a whole fish this way for a customer's wedding. The guests loved it.

SHIITAKE MUSHROOM DUXELLE

- 2 cups shiitake mushrooms or other wild mushrooms
- 1 cup fresh flat-leaf parsley
- 1/2 cup fresh cilantro
- 1 tablespoon chopped garlic
- 1 tablespoon unsalted butter
- 1 tablespoon olive oil

GINGERED CARROT EMULSION

- 4 cups fresh carrot juice
- 1 tablespoon sugar
- 1 teaspoon peeled and minced fresh ginger
- 3/4 cup unsalted butter

- 1 sheet puff pastry, thawed and cut into 4 (6-inch) squares
- 4 (4-ounce) opakapaka fillets or any mild white snapper
- Kosher salt and freshly ground black pepper
- 1 large egg, lightly beaten
- 1 tablespoon unsalted butter
- 2 bunches baby bok choy, halved lengthwise
- 4 fresh cilantro sprigs, for garnish

To prepare the duxelle, in a food processor, combine the mushrooms, parsley, cilantro, and garlic and process until finely pureed. In a sauté pan, add the butter and olive oil and heat over medium-high heat until the butter is just melted. Add the mushroom mixture and cook until all the moisture is absorbed, 5 to 6 minutes. Cover and chill in the refrigerator.

To prepare the carrot sauce, in a small saucepan, add the carrot juice, sugar, and ginger and heat over medium heat until reduced to 1½ cups of liquid, about 12 minutes. Transfer the mixture to a blender, add the butter, and blend until thickened. Keep warm until ready to serve.

To prepare the fish, preheat the oven to 375°. On a clean, dry surface, place the pastry squares. Place 1½ tablespoons of the mushroom mixture in the center of each pastry and top with 1 piece of fish; season with salt and pepper. Wrap the pastry completely around the fish and flip over so the seam is on the bottom. Brush the top of the pastry with the egg. Transfer to a nonstick baking pan and bake until golden brown, 12 to 15 minutes.

Meanwhile, in a skillet, add the butter and melt over high heat, then add the bok choy and sauté until just tender, about 5 minutes.

To serve, ladle enough carrot sauce onto the center of 4 large dinner plates to coat. Place the bok choy in the center of the sauce, top with 1 fish pastry, and garnish each with 1 cilantro sprig.

Crispy-Skin Onaga, Chinese Long Beans, Cake Noodle, and Ginger Beurre Blanc

Serves 4

This is Keith's version of traditional cake noodles—a favorite for many local people—which can be found in every Chinese restaurant in Hawai'i. Again, this is upscale: onaga, which is the best snapper in the world to my taste, long beans, and ginger beurre blanc instead of the usual mixed seafood, vegetables, and oyster sauce. Chinese cake noodles are available in Asian markets; cook them according to package directions.

2 tablespoons vegetable oil

10 ounces Chinese cake noodles, boiled and drained

2 tablespoons plus 1 teaspoon olive oil

4 cups Chinese long beans

1/4 teaspoon sambal (Indonesian chili sauce)

1 teaspoon Asian (toasted) sesame oil

Kosher salt and freshly ground black pepper

1 teaspoon minced shallot

1 teaspoon minced garlic

1 tablespoon peeled and chopped fresh ginger

1/4 cup dry white wine

1 cup unsalted butter, cut into small pieces

4 (4-ounce) onaga (long-tail red snapper) fillets, skin on

1/4 cup Unagi Sauce (page 89)

4 carrot curls, for garnish

In an 8-inch round, nonstick pan, heat the vegetable oil over medium-high heat. Add the noodles and form into a round, 1/2-inch-thick "cake." Cook for 5 minutes per side, until golden brown and crisp. Drain on paper towels, cut into 4 pieces, and set aside.

In a heavy saucepan, add 1 tablespoon of the olive oil and heat over medium-high heat. Add the beans and sauté until just tender, about 5 minutes. Using a slotted spoon, transfer to paper towels to drain. In a large bowl, combine the sambal, sesame oil, and salt and pepper. Add the mixture to the beans and toss to coat the beans evenly. Keep warm until ready to use.

(continued)

continued from page 190

To prepare the beurre blanc, in a small saucepan, heat 1 teaspoon of the olive oil over high heat. Add the shallot, garlic, and ginger and sauté for 3 minutes, until translucent. Add the wine and cook until the liquid is almost evaporated, about 8 minutes. Slowly whisk in the butter until blended. Keep warm until ready to use.

Season the onaga with salt and pepper. In a large sauté pan, heat the remaining 1 tablespoon olive oil over high heat. Add the onaga, skin-side down first, and sear for 4 to 5 minutes per side, until golden brown. Let stand for 3 minutes.

To serve, place 1 piece of cake noodle each in the center of 4 large plates. Divide the beans and place on top of each noodle. Place 1 onaga, skin-side up, to lean against the beans and noodle. Ladle the beurre blanc around the onaga. Drizzle the unagi sauce on top and garnish with the carrot curls.

Steamed Kahuku Farm-Raised Moi, Black Bean Paste, Ong Choy, and Shiitake Nage

Serves 4

Keith's grandma's steamed mullet with black beans was one of his favorite dishes growing up. Now that we have access to a similar fish, moi, he shares one of his best childhood memories with our customers. The light-flavored moi needs a nice light broth like this shiitake nage.

SHIITAKE NAGE

1 tablespoon peanut oil

1 teaspoon minced garlic

1 teaspoon peeled and minced fresh ginger

1/2 cup sliced shiitake mushrooms

1/4 cup plum wine

1 1/2 cups chicken stock

Kosher salt and freshly ground black pepper

4 cups ong choy or other Chinese cabbage

4 (4-ounce) moi (threadfish) fillets or snapper or mullet

2 tablespoons Black Bean Paste (page 83)

1 tablespoon peeled and sliced fresh ginger

1 tablespoon thinly sliced garlic

Kosher salt and freshly ground black pepper

4 tablespoons peanut oil

4 fresh cilantro sprigs, for garnish

To prepare the nage, in a skillet, heat the oil over medium heat. Add the garlic, ginger, and mushrooms and sauté for 4 minutes. Add the plum wine and reduce by half, about 3 minutes. Add the stock and season with salt and pepper. Decrease the heat to low and simmer for 10 minutes, until the flavors have combined. Strain. Cover and refrigerate until ready to use.

Place the ong choy in a bamboo steamer. Place the moi on top. Spread 1/2 tablespoon of the black bean paste on each moi. Top with the ginger and garlic and season with salt and pepper. Steam over high heat for 5 to 6 minutes, until the moi is cooked through. To serve, divide the ong choy and moi and place in the center of 4 bowls. Ladle the reheated nage around each moi. In a small skillet, heat the oil over high heat until it is smoking, then spoon 1 tablespoon on top of each moi. Garnish each with 1 cilantro sprig.

Pan-Seared Moi
with Crispy Oxtail Ravioli

Serves 4

Ivan created this dish for a winemaker's dinner with event hostess Andrea Immer during the 2001 Kapalua Wine and Food Festival. He was bouncing ideas off the wall when this one found him. If you're not familiar with the Japanese curry used in the curry sauce, it can be found at Asian markets in a powder or paste form.

5 pounds oxtail

1/2 cup peanut oil

4 cups diced carrot

1/2 cup diced onion

1/2 cup diced celery

1 teaspoon minced garlic

6 cups beef broth

Kosher salt and freshly ground black pepper

12 (2 by 2-inch) wonton wrappers

1 egg yolk, beaten

1 cup cornstarch

CURRY SAUCE

1 tablespoon vegetable oil

1/2 cup julienned white onion

1/2 cup finely diced carrot

2 teaspoons minced garlic

1 teaspoon peeled and minced fresh ginger

1 medium tomato, diced

2 teaspoons tomato paste

1/4 cup Japanese curry mix

1 teaspoon curry powder

1 teaspoon sugar

4 (4-ounce) moi fillets or any snapper

Kosher salt and freshly ground black pepper

1 tablespoon olive oil

Cottonseed, peanut, or canola oil for deep-frying

1/4 cup micro greens, for garnish

In a large stockpot, heat the oil over high heat, add the oxtail, and cook 6 minutes, until browned. Add the carrot, onion, and celery and sauté until caramelized, about 5 minutes. Add the garlic and sauté for 5 minutes. Add the broth, adding water if more liquid is needed to completely cover. Bring to a boil, then decrease the heat to medium-low and simmer for 2 hours, or until the meat falls off the bone. Remove the oxtail from the pot and let cool before pulling the meat from the bones. Transfer the meat to a large bowl and season with salt and pepper.

To assemble the ravioli, on a clean, dry surface, lay the wonton wrappers. Place 1 teaspoon of meat in the center of each wrapper. Brush the edges with the egg yolk, fold into a triangle, and seal well. Turn each ravioli in the cornstarch to coat lightly. Set aside.

To prepare the curry sauce, in a saucepan, heat the oil over medium-high heat. Add the onion, carrot, garlic, and ginger and sauté until caramelized, about 5 minutes. Add the tomato and tomato paste and cook for 5 minutes, stirring occasionally. Add the Japanese curry, curry powder, sugar, and 6 cups water. Decrease the heat to medium and simmer for 20 minutes, until heated through and all the flavors have combined. Keep warm until ready to use.

Season the moi with salt and pepper. In a sauté pan, heat the olive oil over high heat. Add the moi and sear for 2 minutes per side, for medium doneness.

In a heavy saucepan, pour in the oil to a depth of about 3 inches and heat to 350°. Add the ravioli and fry until golden brown, about 3 minutes. Using a slotted spoon, transfer to paper towels to drain. In a large bowl, toss the ravioli with the curry sauce to coat completely.

To serve, place 3 ravioli in the center of each of 4 plates. Place 1 moi each on top of the ravioli. Top each moi with a quarter of the greens.

Roasted Hawaiian Lehi, Sansei Spicy Crab, Roasted Eggplant and Sweet Potato Tian, and Sweet Carrot Emulsion

Serves 4

We serve this dish because you can get crab-stuffed fish everywhere. But only at Sansei can you get it stuffed with the great spicy crab mixture we use in so many of our sushi rolls. Having the sushi bar really allows our chefs to be creative, because they have access to such great additional ingredients. Lehi is a very mild, soft-flavored fish, so the sauce cannot be overbearing. The sweet carrot emulsion works perfectly.

4 (4-ounce) lehi fillets or any mild snapper

Kosher salt and freshly ground black pepper

1 tablespoon olive oil

3/4 cup Spicy Crab Mix (page 77)

2 long Japanese eggplants, cut lengthwise and thinly sliced

1/2 pound sweet potatoes, boiled and mashed

3 cups fresh carrot juice

1 teaspoon peeled and minced fresh ginger

1 cup unsalted butter

2 tablespoons chopped fresh chives, for garnish

1 tablespoon black sesame seeds, for garnish

Preheat the oven to 375°. Season the lehi with salt and pepper. In a sauté pan, heat the oil over medium-high heat. Add the lehi and sear about 3 minutes per side, until opaque. Top each lehi with 3 tablespoons of the crab mix. Place on a nonstick baking pan and bake for about 7 minutes, until the crab mixture is hot.

Prepare a fire in a charcoal grill or preheat a gas grill. Place the eggplant on the grill rack and grill for 1 minute per side. In 4 round, 3-inch-diameter molds, arrange the eggplant slices to cover the bottom and the sides, reserving some of the eggplant to place on top.

Fill each mold with the potatoes. Top with the reserved eggplant slices to wrap over and completely cover the potatoes. Just before serving, unmold onto a large microwave-safe plate and heat in the microwave for 1 minute.

To prepare the carrot emulsion, in a saucepan, add the carrot juice and ginger, bring to a boil over high heat, and cook until reduced by half, about 5 minutes. Remove from the heat and slowly whisk in the butter until blended. Just before serving, transfer the sauce to a blender and process to thicken, about 1 minute.

Place 1 tian in the center of each of 4 plates. Top each with 1 lehi. Ladle the sauce around the lehi. Top with the chives and sesame seeds.

Miso-Roasted Hapu'upu'u with Honey-Sesame Butter Sauce

Serves 4

Miso-roasted hapu'upu'u is a twist on a local classic, miso butterfish (see our recipe on page 139). Hapu has the same texture as butterfish—but be absolutely sure not to overcook it!

4 (6-ounce) hapu'upu'u fillets or sea
  bass or black cod

2 cups Miso Marinade (page 96)

Kosher salt and freshly ground black
  pepper

1/4 cup packed micro greens

2 cups Honey-Sesame Butter Sauce
  (page 84)

In a shallow dish, combine the hapu and the marinade. Cover and marinate in the refrigerator overnight.

Preheat the oven to 400°. Season the hapu with salt and pepper. Place in a roasting pan and bake for about 12 minutes, until caramelized.

To serve, place a quarter of the greens in the center of each of 4 plates. Top each with 1 hapu and spoon the warmed sauce over all.

Pan-Braised Weke with Anchovy-Tomato Sauce

Serves 4

Ivan's mom used to make weke, also known as goatfish, for him. It's really flaky and, for local kids, it's a real comfort food. Kids would always catch it when fishing, but they never had it with anchovies! Ivan took this dish from his childhood and added an adult twist.

4 small weke or trout, scaled and gutted

Kosher salt and freshly ground black pepper

$1/4$ cup flour

2 tablespoons olive oil

2 tablespoons chopped garlic

1 tablespoon capers

2 tablespoons chopped anchovy

$1/4$ cup Madeira or dry white wine

5 medium vine-ripened tomatoes, chopped

2 cups chicken stock

2 tablespoons tomato paste

$1/2$ cup butter

1 tablespoon truffle oil, for garnish

Season the weke with salt and pepper, then turn in the flour to coat evenly, shaking off the excess. In a sauté pan, heat 1 tablespoon of the oil over medium-high heat. Add the weke and sear for about 2 minutes per side, until medium-rare.

To prepare the sauce, in a large saucepan, heat the remaining 1 tablespoon of oil over medium-high heat. Add the garlic, capers, and anchovy and sauté for 4 minutes. Add the Madeira and reduce by half, about 5 minutes. Add the tomatoes, 1 cup of the stock, and the tomato paste. Decrease the heat to medium and simmer for 5 minutes, until the sauce thickens. Slowly add the remaining 1 cup stock. Add the weke to the broth and simmer for 4 minutes, until the fish is flaky and tender. Remove the weke and set aside. Whisk the butter into the sauce, until thoroughly combined.

To serve, place 1 weke on each of 4 plates. Delicately spoon the sauce on top and drizzle with the truffle oil.

Japanese-Style Jerk Chicken

Serves 4

When we decided to put a chicken dish on the menu, we knew the key was going to be brining the chicken. Now we brine duck, shrimp—all kinds of things. We added shoyu to a jerk spice to turn it Japanese.

2 whole fryers, split in half

2 chili peppers, crushed

1 cup shoyu (Japanese soy sauce)

1 lemon, halved, plus juice of 1 lemon

2 tablespoons shichimi (seven-spice pepper)

$1/4$ cup sake

Juice of 1 lemon

3 cups assorted vegetables (celery, carrots, onions, etc.), cut into 1-inch chunks

$1^1/2$ cups chicken broth

$1^1/2$ tablespoons unsalted butter, at room temperature

Kosher salt and freshly ground black pepper

4 cups Garlic Mashed Potatoes (page 99)

3 tablespoons chopped fresh chives, for garnish

Place the chicken in a shallow dish. In a large bowl, combine the peppers, shoyu, lemon, and 4 cups water. Pour the liquid over the chicken. Cover and marinate in the refrigerator overnight.

Prepare a fire in a charcoal grill or preheat a gas grill. Preheat the oven to 400°. Season the chicken with the shichimi. Place the chicken on the grill rack and sear, skin-side down, for about 4 minutes, until nicely marked. Transfer to an ungreased roasting pan and bake for about 15 minutes, until the skin is brown and crispy and the juices run clear. Remove the chicken from the pan and set aside until ready to use. Set the roasting pan over medium-high heat. Add the sake and lemon juice, stirring to loosen the browned bits from the sides and bottom of the pan. Add the vegetables, decrease the heat to medium, and cook until just tender, about 6 minutes. Add the broth and reduce the liquid by a quarter, about 4 minutes. Stir in the butter and season with salt and pepper.

(continued)

continued from page 199

To serve, divide the mashed potatoes among 4 large serving bowls. Divide the chicken pieces by pulling the breast away from the leg. In each bowl, place a quarter of the chicken on top of the mashed potatoes. Divide the vegetables and place on top of each. Ladle the sauce over all and top with the chives.

Miso-Honey-Marinated Duck Breast with Black Rice Risotto and Yuzu

Serves 4

What else is there to say after "miso honey"? For the black rice risotto, we use Japanese rice instead of the traditional arborio rice for a different and, I think, better texture. Black rice is a medium-grain, unmilled rice native to Indonesia and the Philippines with a wonderfully nutty taste; it can be found at some Asian markets and at natural food stores.

4 (6-ounce) duck breasts

2 tablespoons white miso (soybean paste)

3 tablespoons honey

1 tablespoon kosher salt

1 tablespoon sugar

1 tablespoon olive oil

1/2 cup finely chopped onion

1 tablespoon minced garlic

1 cup Japanese short-grain rice

1/2 cup black rice

1/4 cup dry white wine

4 cups chicken stock

1/2 cup unsalted butter

1/2 cup loosely packed spinach

1/2 cup micro greens

1/2 cup Yuzu Butter Sauce (page 87)

Place the duck in a shallow dish. In a large bowl, mix the miso, honey, salt, sugar, and enough water to cover the duck. Pour the liquid over the duck and marinate in the refrigerator for 4 hours.

To prepare the risotto, in a saucepan, heat the oil over medium-high heat. Add the onion and garlic and sauté for 5 minutes, until translucent. Add the Japanese rice and black rice and cook for 1 minute, then add the wine, stirring to combine well. Slowly add the chicken stock, 1 cup at a time. Whisk in the butter until combined. Add the spinach, decrease the heat to low, and cook, covered, for 15 minutes, until the rice is light and fluffy. Set aside and keep warm until ready to serve.

Preheat the oven to 400°. Remove the duck from the marinade and gently pat dry with a towel. Heat an ovenproof sauté pan over medium-high heat. Add the duck, reduce the temperature to low, and cook, skin-side down, until the skin is caramelized, about 4 minutes. Turn once and cook for 4 minutes. Carefully transfer the pan to the oven and bake for 10 minutes, until cooked through. Let cool slightly, then slice.

To serve, divide the risotto into 4 bowls. Top each with a quarter of the sliced duck and sprinkle the greens on top. Drizzle the warmed sauce over all.

Smoked Maple Leaf Duck Breast with Japanese Eggplant and Plum Wine

Serves 4

Summertime is barbecue time no matter where you live. We developed this grilled dish for one of our summer menus.

1 tablespoon kosher salt

1 teaspoon dried tarragon

3 tablespoons honey

4 (6-ounce) duck breasts

4 cups plum wine

3 tablespoons Veal Demi-Glace (page 95)

3 tablespoons unsalted butter, cold and cut into cubes

1 tablespoon olive oil

2 Japanese eggplants, cut diagonally into $1/2$-inch-thick slices

$1/2$ cup micro greens, for garnish

In a large bowl, combine the salt, tarragon, honey, and 4 cups water. Place the duck in the brine and marinate for 4 hours in the refrigerator. Remove the duck and gently pat dry with a towel. Set aside.

In a bowl, soak ½ cup applewood chips in water for about 10 minutes. Drain and place the chips in a large pot that you don't mind getting messy. Lay a piece of aluminum foil on top of the chips and cover the pot. Heat the chips over high heat until smoking. Remove from the heat and place the duck on top of the foil. Cover and smoke for 5 minutes.

In a saucepan, add the plum wine and cook over high heat until reduced by two-thirds, about 8 minutes. Add the demi-glace and then immediately whisk in the butter. Keep warm until ready to serve.

Preheat the oven to 350°. Heat an ovenproof sauté pan over medium-high heat. When the pan is hot, decrease the heat to low, add the duck, skin-side down, and sear until the skin is caramelized, 3 to 4 minutes. Transfer the pan to the oven and bake for 5 minutes.

In a skillet, heat the oil over medium-high heat. Add the eggplant and sauté until golden brown, about 3 minutes.

To serve, place a quarter of the eggplant in the center of each of 4 plates. Slice the duck and place the slices on top of the eggplant on each plate. Ladle the sauce over all and top with the greens.

Mild Chili and Porcini–Dusted Beef Filet, Garlic Mashed Potatoes, and Shiitake Mushroom with Unagi Demi-Glace

Serves 4

When we first opened the Kapalua restaurant, we needed a meat dish for the menu. Of course, there's no better cut of beef than filet. So we added the unagi demi-glace and created a Japanese filet. You can find the mushroom powder in gourmet groceries or Italian markets.

$1/4$ cup porcini mushroom powder

1 teaspoon shichimi (seven-spice pepper)

1 teaspoon sugar

4 (6-ounce) beef tenderloin filets, trimmed

1 tablespoon olive oil

1 cup sliced fresh shiitake mushrooms

3 cups Garlic Mashed Potatoes (page 99)

1 cup Unagi Demi-Glace (page 96)

2 tablespoons chopped fresh chives, for garnish

In a small bowl, mix together the mushroom powder, shichimi, and sugar until well combined. Sprinkle both sides of the beef filets with the mixture. In a large skillet, heat the oil over medium-high heat. Add the beef and sear for $4\frac{1}{2}$ minutes per side for medium doneness. Halfway through cooking the beef, add the mushrooms to the skillet and sauté for 4 to 5 minutes.

To serve, spoon a quarter of the potatoes in the center of each of 4 plates. Place 1 beef filet on top of the potatoes and pour $1/4$ cup of the warmed demi-glace over the filet. Top with the mushrooms and chives.

Braised Short Ribs
with Spicy Thai Curry Sauce

Serves 4

This dish grew out of a desire to do something spicy and something different with short ribs. For Sansei that meant, of course, adding an Asian flair. The fresh herbs provide the perfect endnote.

$1/4$ cup vegetable oil

4 (3-bone) 3-inch short ribs, about
    2 pounds total

1 cup diced carrot

$1/2$ cup diced onion

$1/2$ cup chopped celery

4 peeled whole garlic cloves

8 cups beef stock

SPICY THAI CURRY SAUCE

$1/4$ cup vegetable oil

1 teaspoon peeled and minced fresh
    ginger

1 teaspoon minced garlic

$1/2$ cup fresh cilantro stems

1 tablespoon red Thai curry paste

1 teaspoon curry powder

2 tablespoons paprika

3 tablespoons tomato paste

1 cup sake

3 cups coconut milk

2 tablespoons sugar

1 tablespoon fish sauce (patis)

1 teaspoon freshly squeezed lemon
    juice

Kosher salt and freshly ground black
    pepper

$1/4$ cup fresh mint leaves, for garnish

$1/2$ cup fresh cilantro leaves, for garnish

$1/2$ cup fresh Thai basil leaves,
    for garnish

$1/2$ cup dry-roasted peanuts, for
    garnish

In a saucepan, heat the oil over high heat. Add the short ribs and sauté for 3 to 4 minutes, until browned. Add the carrot, onion, celery, garlic, and beef stock and stir to combine. Simmer for 2 hours, or until the ribs are fork-tender. Remove from the heat and set aside.

To make the sauce, in a saucepan, heat the oil over medium heat. Add the ginger, garlic, and cilantro stems and sauté for 2 to 3 minutes, until tender. Add the curry paste, curry powder, paprika, and tomato paste and stir to combine. Add the sake and cook, stirring, until the liquid is reduced by half, about 5 minutes. Add the coconut milk, sugar, fish sauce, and lemon juice, mixing well, and cook for 10 minutes. Strain through a fine-mesh sieve and return the sauce to the pan. Season with salt and pepper. Add the short ribs and simmer over low heat for 15 minutes, to let the flavors combine.

To serve, divide the ribs among 4 bowls and ladle the sauce over the ribs. Top with the mint, cilantro, basil, and peanuts.

Beef Tenderloin On Udon Noodles with Demi-Glace

Serves 4

In Napa Valley, I tasted a dish made with big, curly pasta, rabbit, and a really nice demi-glace. I brought it home, where we use udon noodles, filet of beef, and veal demi-glace. Definitely uptown Japanese!

1 cup Veal Demi-Glace (page 95)

1 cup thinly sliced shiitake mushrooms

2 tablespoons unsalted butter, cold

1 tablespoon porcini mushroom powder

1 tablespoon Korean chili pepper powder

4 (8-ounce) beef tenderloin filets, trimmed

Kosher salt and freshly ground black pepper

2 tablespoons olive oil

1 1/2 pounds udon noodles, boiled and drained

1/2 cup freshly grated Parmesan cheese

1/4 cup finely chopped green onion, green part only, for garnish

In a small saucepan, combine the demi-glace and mushrooms and bring to a simmer over medium heat, about 5 minutes. Remove from the heat and whisk in the butter until smooth. Set aside and keep the sauce warm until ready to use.

In a small bowl, combine the mushroom powder and chili powder. Sprinkle both sides of the beef filets with the mixture. Season with salt and pepper. In an ovenproof sauté pan, heat the olive oil over medium-high heat, add the beef, and sear for about 3 minutes per side, until browned. Transfer the pan to the oven and bake for 5 minutes for medium doneness. Keep warm until ready to serve.

To serve, add the noodles and cheese to the sauce and toss well to combine. Divide among 4 bowls. Slice each beef filet into 5 or 6 pieces and fan the slices on top of the noodles. Top with the green onion.

Gorgonzola-Stuffed Filet, Wild Mushroom Ragout, Maui Onion Demi-Glace, and Okinawan Sweet Potato Mousse

Serves 4

I think filet of beef needs to have body added to it. So instead of a Gorgonzola sauce, why not stuff the meat with the cheese? The demi-glace and the mousse balance the sharpness of the Gorgonzola.

MAUI ONION DEMI-GLACE

3 tablespoons unsalted butter

2 cups julienned Maui onion or other sweet onion

3 cups Veal Demi-Glace (page 95)

4 cups red wine

Kosher salt and freshly ground black pepper

4 (4-ounce) beef tenderloin filets

4 ounces Gorgonzola cheese, crumbled (about 1 cup)

Kosher salt and freshly ground black pepper

3 tablespoons olive oil

4 tablespoons unsalted butter, at room temperature

4 cups sliced wild mushrooms, such as shiitake, oyster, portobello, or chanterelle

1 tablespoon minced garlic

1/4 cup chicken stock

1 pound Okinawan sweet potatoes or yams, peeled and diced

1/4 cup heavy cream

1 teaspoon peeled and minced fresh ginger

To prepare the demi-glace, in a large skillet, heat 1 tablespoon of the butter over medium heat. Add the onion and cook for about 12 minutes, until it's a rich brown color and intensely sweet. Add the demi-glace, wine, and the remaining 2 tablespoons of butter and stir until well combined. Season with salt and pepper. Keep warm until ready to use.

(continued)

continued from page 207

Into the side of each beef filet, slice a pocket about 2 inches deep. Stuff each pocket with 1 ounce of cheese and season the filets with salt and pepper. In a sauté pan, heat 2 tablespoons of the oil over high heat. Add the beef and sear for 3 minutes per side. Let stand for 4 minutes.

In a large sauté pan, heat the remaining 1 tablespoon olive oil and 2 tablespoons of the butter over high heat. Add the mushrooms and garlic and sauté for 3 minutes. Add the stock and cook until all the liquid has been absorbed, about 4 minutes. Keep warm until ready to serve.

Place the potatoes in a medium stockpot and add water to cover. Bring to a boil over high heat and cook for 20 minutes, until fork-tender. Drain. In a small saucepan, bring the cream just to a boil over medium heat, then remove from the heat. In a bowl, using a potato masher, mash the potatoes, cream, the remaining 2 tablespoons butter, and ginger until creamy. Season with salt and pepper.

To serve, spoon a mound of the potatoes in the center of each of 4 plates. Top each with 1 filet. Spoon the mushrooms on top and ladle the demi-glace over all.

Sweet Plates

Mom's Brownies

Makes 24 to 48 brownies

Boy, talk about the best. These are the brownies I grew up with. Whenever I taste a brownie, this is the one to which I compare it. It's all a brownie should be: chewy, nutty, and chocolaty. For me, there's nothing like Mom's brownies. We use Ghirardelli, but any good-quality cocoa is fine.

1 1/2 cups unsalted butter, at room temperature

2 cups cocoa powder

4 cups sugar

8 eggs, lightly beaten

3 cups flour

2 teaspoons baking powder

2 teaspoons salt

2 cups chopped nuts, any kind

1 cup macadamia nuts, chopped

Preheat the oven to 350°. Butter a 12 by 18-inch jelly-roll pan or a baking sheet with sides. In a saucepan, combine the butter and cocoa powder over medium heat, stirring until melted and combined. In a large bowl, combine the sugar and eggs. Add the cocoa mixture and mix gently. Into another bowl, sift the flour, baking powder, and salt and add, a little at a time, to the wet ingredients, mixing until incorporated. Fold in the nuts. Pour the batter into the prepared pan and bake for about 30 minutes, checking periodically, until a toothpick inserted in the center comes out clean. Let cool, then cut into bars or squares.

Oatmeal Cake

Makes 15 squares

My mom first tasted this cake at a friend's barbecue party many years ago. As is typical in Hawai'i, great recipes spread like wildfire throughout the community. Also typically, everyone modifies "found" recipes to suit their own and their family's tastes. In this case, Mom decreased the sugar, added macadamia nuts to the topping, and changed the shape of the cake to call it her own.

1 cup old-fashioned oats

1 1/2 cups boiling water

1 cup granulated sugar

1 cup lightly packed brown sugar

2 eggs

1/2 cup unsalted butter, at room temperature

1 1/3 cups flour

1 teaspoon ground cinnamon

1 teaspoon baking soda

1 teaspoon salt

TOPPING

6 tablespoons unsalted butter, melted

1/4 cup evaporated milk

1/2 cup lightly packed brown sugar

1/2 teaspoon vanilla extract

1 cup sweetened shredded coconut

1 cup walnuts, chopped

1 cup macadamia nuts, chopped

Preheat the oven to 350°. Grease a 13 by 9-inch baking pan. In a bowl, mix together the oats and boiling water and let stand for 20 minutes. In a large bowl, combine the sugar, brown sugar, eggs, and butter. Add the flour, cinnamon, baking soda, and salt, stirring until well combined. Pour the batter into the prepared pan. Bake for 30 minutes, until a cake tester comes out clean.

Meanwhile, in a bowl, combine the topping ingredients and mix well. Set aside.

Increase the oven setting to heat the broiler. When the cake is slightly cooled, spread the topping on the cake. Place under the broiler for about 1½ minutes, until the topping starts to bubble and turn golden brown. Let cool, then cut into 3 by 2½-inch squares.

Pound Cake

Makes 24 slices

For my family, this is real comfort food. It's my dad's favorite, and my mom makes sure to have it in the house at all times. And now she bakes one for the Honolulu restaurant every morning. Even in the warm, humid climate of Hawai'i, you can keep it under a cake dome for at least a week. Of course, it never lasts a week, either in the restaurant or in our house.

2 1/4 cups flour

1 3/4 cups sugar

1 cup unsalted butter, at roomtemperature

3 eggs

8 ounces sour cream

1 teaspoon vanilla extract

1/2 teaspoon baking soda

Confectioners' sugar, for dusting (optional)

Preheat the oven to 350°. Spray a Bundt pan generously with nonstick cooking spray. In the bowl of an electric mixer, combine all the ingredients and beat on high speed for about 2 minutes, until the batter pulls away from the sides of the bowl. Pour the batter into the prepared pan and bake for 45 minutes, until a toothpick inserted in the cake comes out clean. Invert immediately onto a plate. Dust with confectioners' sugar, if desired, for a more festive look. Slice and serve.

Granny Smith Apple Tart

Serves 4

It's been on the menu since Day One, and it's still there. It includes everything a dessert needs to be great: pastry, ice cream, and a caramel sauce so good that I've seen some of our customers drink it out of a glass! The puff pastry can be cut into circles with a cookie cutter, an inverted drinking glass, or anything else circular—or it can be cut into squares, too, if that would be easier.

CARAMEL SAUCE

2 cups sugar

2 cups heavy cream

1 cup unsalted butter

4 sheets puff pastry, cut into 5-inch-diameter circles

1 egg, beaten

1 large Granny Smith apple, cored and thinly sliced

1 tablespoon sugar

1 tablespoon ground cinnamon

Vanilla Bean Ice Cream (page 223)

To make the sauce, in a saucepan, combine the sugar and 1 cup water and cook over medium-high heat, stirring, until the sugar caramelizes and turns dark amber in color. Mix in the cream. Whisk in the butter until smooth. Keep warm until ready to use. Or, it can be prepared ahead of time and stored in an airtight container in the refrigerator for several days; reheat before using.

Preheat the oven to 375°. Grease a baking sheet. Transfer the puff pastry to the prepared baking sheet. Brush each with the egg and top with the apples. In a small bowl, combine the sugar and cinnamon and sprinkle the mixture over each pastry. Bake for 10 minutes, until the pastry rises and is golden brown. Top each with a scoop of the ice cream and serve with the caramel sauce.

Traditional Burnt Crème

Serves 6

You gotta have chocolate. You gotta have pastry. You gotta have ice cream. And you gotta have crème brûlée. It may surprise you to have the best you've ever tasted come from a Japanese restaurant!

> 2 cups heavy cream
>
> 4 egg yolks
>
> $^1/_2$ cup plus 3 tablespoons sugar
>
> 2 tablespoons pure vanilla extract

In a saucepan, heat the cream over low heat until bubbles start to form around the edge of the pan, about 6 minutes. In the bowl of an electric mixer set on medium-high speed, beat together the egg yolks and $^1/_2$ cup of the sugar until the mixture has doubled in volume, about 3 minutes. Whisk in a small amount of the warmed cream, making sure the temperature of the egg mixture does not rise too rapidly. Add the remaining cream to the egg mixture. Stir in the vanilla.

Preheat the oven to 300°. Place 6 ramekins in a high-sided baking pan on a rack pulled slightly out of the oven. Divide the cream mixture evenly among the ramekins. Fill the pan with hot water to reach about halfway up the sides of the ramekins. Carefully slide the rack back into the oven. Bake until the custard has set, about 45 minutes. Remove from the oven and let cool in the water, then remove the ramekins. Cover and chill in the refrigerator for at least 3 to 4 hours before serving.

Just before serving, sprinkle $^1/_2$ tablespoon of sugar on top of each custard, covering the entire surface. Using a lit butane torch, carefully caramelize the sugar. Alternatively, place the ramekins on a baking sheet and slip under a hot broiler just long enough to caramelize the sugar. Watch closely, as they burn easily. Serve immediately.

Tempura Fried Ice Cream

Serves 4

Hot ice cream? Go figure. Lots of restaurants have hot ice cream desserts, but nothing works like pound cake for this dessert. We've found it also tastes great with green tea ice cream.

20 thin slices frozen pound cake

2 cups Vanilla Bean Ice Cream (page 223), formed into 4 balls

Cottonseed, peanut, or canola oil for deep-frying

2 cups tempura batter

1/2 cup chocolate sauce

1 teaspoon white sesame seeds, toasted (page 16), for garnish

Place a 1-foot square of plastic wrap on a clean, dry surface. Arrange 3 slices of cake, overlapping vertically, on the plastic wrap. Lay 2 more slices horizontally on the top and bottom of the 3 vertical slices. Place 1 ice cream ball in the center of the cake slices. Cover the ice cream with the remaining cake, arranging the slices in the same configuration as before. Gather the corners of the plastic wrap at the top and twist to hold the cake and ice cream firmly. Repeat with the remaining cake slices and ice cream, to make a total of 4 balls. Freeze for at least 2 hours, or up to 1 week as long as they're tightly wrapped.

In a wok or deep, heavy saucepan, pour in the oil to a depth of about 4 inches and heat to 350°. Unwrap each cake ball and dip in the tempura batter to coat completely. Using a slotted spoon, carefully transfer each ball to the oil. Fry for 2 to 3 minutes, or until crisp and golden brown. Using a slotted spoon, transfer to paper towels to drain.

To serve, place 1 fried ball in the center of each of 4 plates. Drizzle the chocolate sauce on top and sprinkle the sesame seeds over all.

'Ulupalakua Strawberry Martini with Vanilla Bean Gelato and Chocolate Lumpia

Serves 4

'Ulupalakua is an area of "upcountry" Maui on the slopes of Mt. Haleakalä. The cool climate produces strawberries—as well as lots of other agricultural products—with strong and vibrant flavor and color. This dessert was created to make optimum use of those berries. Of course, any excellent strawberries available in your area may be substituted.

VANILLA BEAN GELATO

- 2 1/4 cups whole milk
- 1 vanilla bean, split lengthwise and seeded
- 1/3 cup heavy cream
- 10 tablespoons superfine granulated sugar
- 4 large egg yolks

CHOCOLATE LUMPIA

- 4 lumpia wrappers
- 4 medium-size Milky Way bars or any candy bar, cut into 3-inch-long pieces
- 1 egg, beaten
- Cottonseed, peanut, or canola oil for deep-frying
- 1 1/2 pints fresh strawberries, hulled and sliced
- 1/4 cup plus 1 teaspoon sugar
- 3/4 cup cognac or brandy
- 4 fresh mint sprigs

To make the gelato, in a 2-quart heavy saucepan, bring the milk, vanilla bean, cream, and 5 tablespoons of the sugar just to a simmer over medium-low heat, stirring until the sugar is dissolved. In the bowl of an electric mixer, beat the yolks and the remaining 5 tablespoons sugar until the mixture is thick and pale. Add the milk mixture in a slow stream, whisking constantly. Pour the mixture into a saucepan and cook over medium-low heat, stirring constantly, until a thermometer registers 170 degrees. Do not allow to boil. Pour the custard through a sieve into a metal bowl set in a large bowl of ice and cold water. Allow to cool completely in the ice bath, then cover and chill in the refrigerator until cold. Transfer to an ice cream machine and process and freeze according to manufacturer's instructions.

To make the lumpia, on a clean, dry surface, lay the wrappers with 1 corner facing you. Place the candy bar pieces crosswise in the middle of each wrapper. Roll from the bottom, jelly-roll style, enclosing the candy bar, then fold in the side corners. Brush the remaining edge with the egg and seal, making sure there are no gaps in the wrapper. Freeze until the candy bar is firm, about 2 hours.

In a heavy saucepan, pour in the oil to a depth of about 4 inches and heat to 350°. Add the lumpia and fry, turning with tongs to cook evenly, for 2 to 3 minutes, until crisp. The candy should still be firm. Using a slotted spoon, transfer to paper towels to drain and set aside until ready to use.

In a nonreactive bowl, combine the strawberries and 1 teaspoon of the sugar and marinate for 10 minutes, until the sugar dissolves and a strawberry syrup forms. Drain, reserving the syrup, and set aside.

In a heavy saucepan, combine the cognac, the remaining ¼ cup of sugar, and the reserved strawberry syrup. Simmer over medium heat until the sugar is dissolved and the liquid thickens slightly and is reduced by a quarter, 5 to 8 minutes. Let cool before using.

To serve, divide the strawberries evenly among 4 large martini glasses and top with 2 small scoops of the gelato. Garnish each with 1 lumpia, a drizzle of the cognac syrup, and 1 mint sprig.

Chocolate Macadamia Nut Pie

Serves 8

This recipe is a twist on the American classics Derby Pie and Jeff Davis Pie, substituting macadamia nuts (we're in Hawai'i, right?) for the pecans and walnuts and spiced rum for the bourbon.

> 2 tablespoons flour
>
> 1/2 cup granulated sugar
>
> 1/2 cup brown sugar, firmly packed
>
> 1/2 cup corn syrup
>
> 4 eggs
>
> 3 tablespoons spiced rum
>
> 1/2 cup semisweet chocolate chips
>
> 1/2 cup chopped macadamia nuts
>
> 1 (9-inch) pie shell

Preheat the oven to 450°. In a bowl, sift together the flour, sugar, and brown sugar. Add the corn syrup, eggs, and rum and mix gently until combined, being careful not to overmix.

Spread the chocolate chips and macadamia nuts in the bottom of the pie shell. Pour in the filling and bake for 10 minutes. Decrease the temperature to 350° and continue baking until the filling is firm, about 30 minutes. Serve warm or at room temperature.

Pineapple Rum Crisps

Serves 4 to 6

"Weddle" plates were created by our "calabash cousin," pastry chef Rodney Weddle, to complement our food. This is one of those really good, solid, "workhorse" desserts that everyone needs in their dessert repertoire. It's great served hot with ice cream and is delicious served cold, too. Of course, the pineapples we get here are just incredible, especially the Maui pineapples, which make the whole dessert. If you don't have access to fresh Hawaiian pineapple, be sure to get the best fruit you can find.

TOPPING

1 cup all-purpose flour

1 cup old-fashioned oats

3/4 cup light brown sugar

1 teaspoon ground cinnamon

3/4 cup unsalted butter, cut into small chunks

1/4 cup unsalted butter

4 cups diced fresh pineapple

1/3 cup dark brown sugar

1/4 cup granulated sugar

1/4 cup dark rum

Confectioners' sugar, for dusting

Preheat the oven to 375°. To make the topping, in a bowl, stir together the flour, oats, sugar, and cinnamon. Using a pastry blender or two knives, cut the butter into the dry ingredients until the mixture has the consistency of coarse meal. Set aside.

In a large sauté pan, melt the butter over low heat. Add the pineapple and sauté over medium heat for 2 minutes. Add the brown sugar, sugar, and rum and cook until the sugar has dissolved. Remove from the heat and divide among 4 to 6 ramekins, each about 4 inches in diameter (or an equivalent size). Sprinkle the topping evenly over the pineapple in each ramekin. Transfer the ramekins to a baking sheet and bake for 30 to 40 minutes, until the top is golden brown and the filling is bubbly. Dust the top of each crisp with the confectioners' sugar. Serve warm with whipped cream or ice cream.

Individual Bittersweet Truffle Cakes with Vanilla Bean Ice Cream and Chocolate Wafers

Serves 6

Rodney first tried this dessert at a culinary event on Maui, where he was teamed with Chef Dean Fearing of the Mansion on Turtle Creek in Dallas. Since then, he's perfected his version of what has become a very popular dish. It's a great ending to any meal and it's also a chocolate lover's ideal dessert. There's no better match, of course, than chocolate and vanilla.

VANILLA BEAN ICE CREAM

- 4 cups half-and-half
- 1 vanilla bean, split lengthwise and seeded
- 10 egg yolks
- 1 1/3 cup sugar

CHOCOLATE WAFERS

- 1 cup flour
- 1 tablespoon cocoa powder
- 1/2 cup unsalted butter
- 1 cup confectioners' sugar
- 3 egg whites

TRUFFLE CAKE

- Flour for dusting
- 7 tablespoons unsalted butter
- 7 ounces bittersweet chocolate
- 2 1/2 ounces unsweetened chocolate
- 3/4 cup sugar
- 2 tablespoons cornstarch
- 2 eggs plus 2 egg yolks
- 1 tablespoon Grand Marnier

- Confectioners' sugar, for dusting

To make the ice cream, in a saucepan, bring the half-and-half and vanilla bean to a boil over high heat. In a bowl, whisk the egg yolks with the sugar. Add a little of the half-and-half mixture to the egg mixture and stir to combine, but make sure the temperature of the egg mixture does not rise too rapidly. Then add the egg mixture to the half-and-half mixture. Cook, stirring, over medium heat until the mixture thickens enough to coat the back of a wooden spoon. Strain through a fine-mesh sieve and cool to room temperature. Cover and refrigerate until completely cool. Then transfer to an ice cream machine and process and freeze according to manufacturer's instructions.

To make the wafers, preheat the oven to 400°. Line a baking sheet with parchment paper. In a bowl, sift together the flour and cocoa powder; set aside. In an electric mixer with the paddle attachment, cream the butter and sugar on medium speed. With the mixer on low speed, add the cocoa powder mixture until combined. Slowly mix in the egg whites, mixing until smooth. Drop the batter by tablespoonfuls onto the prepared sheet, and with a small spatula spread the batter into 2-inch disks, about $\frac{1}{8}$-inch thick. Bake for 5 to 8 minutes, until crisp. Set aside until ready to use.

To make the cake, preheat the oven to 350°. Butter six 4-ounce ramekins and dust with flour, shaking off any excess. In a saucepan, melt the butter over low heat. Add the bitter-sweet and unsweetened chocolates and stir until melted and smooth. Set aside. In an electric mixer with the whip attachment, combine the sugar, cornstarch, eggs, egg yolks, and Grand Marnier and mix on low speed until smooth. Add the chocolate mixture and mix on low speed until combined. Spoon $\frac{1}{2}$ cup of batter into each prepared ramekin. Transfer the ramekins to a baking sheet and bake for 12 to 15 minutes, until the cake rises about $1\frac{1}{2}$ inches above the rim of the ramekin. The centers should be soft.

To serve, remove the cakes from the ramekins and place 1 onto each of 6 plates. Top with the ice cream. Place 1 wafer on top of the ice cream and sprinkle confectioners' sugar over all.

Macadamia Nut Crunch Cake with Chocolate Sorbet

Serves 4 to 6

This is a somewhat off-the-wall dessert that Rodney came up with during a highly creative streak. Although it's unusual, the flavors and textures work very well together. The crunch of the macadamia nuts and the meringue combine beautifully with the smooth bittersweet chocolate sorbet. As a twist on the European tradition of ground almonds, we use ground macadamia nuts to give the dish its Island flair.

SORBET SYRUP

4 cups water

2 cups sugar

$1/2$ cup corn syrup

CHOCOLATE SORBET

2 cups Sorbet Syrup (above)

9 ounces unsweetened chocolate, finely chopped

5 ounces bittersweet chocolate, finely chopped

$1/4$ cup freshly squeezed orange juice

$1/4$ cup freshly squeezed lemon juice

MERINGUE DISCS

1 cup ground macadamia nuts

1 cup confectioners' sugar

$1/4$ cup flour

3 egg whites

$1/3$ cup granulated sugar

$2 1/2$ tablespoons brown sugar

CHOCOLATE MOUSSE

15 ounces bittersweet chocolate

$1/2$ cup milk

3 cups heavy cream, lightly whipped

PRALINE CRUNCH

11 ounces white chocolate

$1 1/3$ cups hazelnut paste

$2 1/2$ cups corn flakes, toasted

Chocolate shavings, for garnish

Macadamia nuts, for garnish

To make the sorbet syrup, in a saucepan, combine the water, sugar, and corn syrup and bring to a boil over high heat. Set aside to cool.

To make the sorbet, in a saucepan, bring the cooled sorbet syrup and 1 cup water to a boil over high heat. Add the unsweetened and bittersweet chocolates, decrease the heat to low, and stir until completely melted. Remove from the heat and stir in the orange and lemon juices. Strain and chill. Transfer to an ice cream machine and process and freeze according to manufacturer's instructions.

To make the meringue discs, preheat the oven to 300°. Line a baking sheet with parchment paper. In a bowl, sift the macadamia nuts, confectioners' sugar, and flour. Set aside. In an electric mixer on high speed and using the whip attachment, whip the egg whites until foamy. Add the sugar and brown sugar, a little at a time, and with the mixer on high speed, whip until stiff peaks form. Carefully fold the flour mixture into the egg white mixture. Spoon the mixture into a pastry bag fitted with a ¼-inch tip and pipe 3-inch circles onto the prepared baking sheet. Bake for 30 to 40 minutes, until crisp and lightly browned.

To make the mousse, in a double boiler, melt the chocolate over low heat. Remove from the heat and stir in the milk. Gently fold in the whipped cream. Cover and let stand at room temperature for up to 1 hour, or refrigerate and remove from the refrigerator and let stand for 1 hour before using.

To make the praline crunch, in a double boiler, melt the white chocolate over low heat. Remove from the heat and mix in the nut paste. Gently fold in the corn flakes. Set aside.

To assemble the cakes, place four to six 3-inch stainless steel or PVC rings on a parchment-lined baking sheet. Place a meringue disc on the bottom of each ring. Scoop 2 tablespoons of praline crunch on top of the meringue. Top with the mousse and level off with a spatula. Freeze until set, about 30 minutes.

To serve, remove the cakes from the rings and place 1 cake in the center of each plate. Top with the chocolate shavings. Arrange 3 small scoops of chocolate sorbet around each cake and sprinkle with the macadamia nuts.

Fallen Soufflé with Waimea Strawberries and Vanilla Ice Cream

Serves 4 to 6

Rodney had the privilege of working at the Kahala Mandarin Oriental Hotel in Honolulu with one of the world's best contemporary chefs, Oliver Altherr, who is as talented in pastry as he is in cooking. He helped Rodney create this dessert. It's a little bit complicated to prepare, but the result is awesome.

SOUFFLÉ BATTER

- 4 cups heavy cream
- 8 cups milk
- 10 tablespoons unsalted butter
- 1 vanilla bean, split lengthwise and seeded
- 13/4 cups sugar, plus additional for dusting
- 1 teaspoon salt
- 13/4 cups bread flour

- 12 egg yolks
- 6 egg whites

- 2 1/4 cups sugar
- 2 cups Waimea strawberries, hulled and quartered
- 1/4 cup strawberry puree
- 2 tablespoons lemon juice
- Vanilla Bean Ice Cream (page 223)
- Confectioners' sugar, for dusting

Preheat the oven to 400°. To make the soufflé batter, in a large saucepan, combine the cream, milk, butter, and vanilla bean and bring to a boil over high heat. Cook for 20 to 30 minutes, until the mixture is reduced to 8 cups of liquid. Decrease the heat to medium and add 1¼ cups of the sugar and the salt, stirring until dissolved. Add the flour and stir until combined. Add the egg yolks and continue cooking until the mixture resembles a thick paste. Remove from the heat and transfer to an electric mixer with the paddle attachment. On medium speed, mix until the mixture cools down to room temperature. Keep refrigerated until ready to use.

Butter the sides of 4 to 6 ramekins and dust each with sugar. In an electric mixer on high speed and using the whip attachment, whisk the egg whites until foamy. Gradually add the remaining $\frac{1}{2}$ cup of sugar and whip until stiff peaks form. Fold the egg whites into the batter, mixing until combined.

To prepare the caramel, in a saucepan, combine the 2 $\frac{1}{4}$ cups sugar and $\frac{1}{2}$ cup water over low heat. Cook for 10 to 12 minutes, until dark amber in color.

Place the ramekins in a high-sided baking pan on a rack pulled slightly out of the oven. Divide the caramel evenly among the prepared ramekins. Divide the soufflé batter among the ramekins. Fill the pan with hot water to reach about halfway up the sides of the ramekins. Carefully slide the rack back into the oven. Bake for 35 to 40 minutes, until firm. Remove from the oven and remove the ramekins from the water bath, setting aside to cool.

In a bowl, toss the strawberries, puree, and lemon juice until combined. Set aside until ready to use.

To serve, if necessary, reheat the soufflés in the microwave for 1 minute or in a 350° oven until heated through, 4 to 7 minutes. Remove each one onto a serving plate. Spoon the strawberries around each soufflé. Scoop vanilla ice cream on the sides of the soufflés and dust each one with confectioners' sugar.

Fried Truffles with Kona Coffee Ice Cream

Serves 4 to 6

Rodney is always trying to invent unique petit fours—that little something sweet to serve after dinner that's nontraditional, unconventional. This is one of those "little somethings." Since the truffles are served hot, the ice cream melts over them and blends with the chocolate.

KONA COFFEE ICE CREAM

4 cups half-and-half

¹/₄ cup whole Kona coffee beans

10 egg yolks

1 ¹/₂ cups sugar

TRUFFLES

16 ounces bittersweet chocolate, chopped

1 cup heavy cream

2 cups panko (Japanese breadcrumbs)

2 eggs, beaten

Cottonseed, peanut, or canola oil for deep-frying

1 teaspoon ground cinnamon

1 cup sugar

Confectioners' sugar, for dusting

To make the ice cream, in a bowl, combine the half-and-half with the coffee beans. Cover and refrigerate for 1 to 2 days, until the coffee flavor is strong. Strain the mixture into a saucepan and bring to a boil over medium heat. In a bowl, whisk together the egg yolks and sugar. Add a little of the half-and-half mixture to the egg mixture and stir to combine, but make sure the temperature of the egg mixture does not rise too rapidly. Transfer the egg mixture to the saucepan and cook until the mixture thickens enough to coat the back of a wooden spoon. Remove from the heat and let cool to room temperature. Cover and refrigerate to cool completely. Then transfer to an ice cream machine and process and freeze according to manufacturer's instructions.

To make the truffles, place the chocolate in a heatproof bowl. In a saucepan, bring the cream to a boil over medium heat. Remove from the heat and pour over the chocolate, stirring until smooth. Refrigerate until firm. Pour the panko into a shallow dish. Using a small ice cream scoop or melon baller, scoop out round balls of the truffle mix. Dip into the egg, then roll in the panko. Repeat with the remaining truffle mixture. Freeze the truffles for 2 hours. In a heavy saucepan, pour in the oil to a depth of about 2 inches and heat to 350°. Carefully drop the truffles into the oil and fry for 30 to 45 seconds, until browned. Using a slotted spoon, transfer to paper towels to drain. In a bowl, mix the cinnamon and sugar. Roll each truffle in the cinnamon sugar.

To serve, place 3 truffles in the center of each bowl. Top with the ice cream and dust with the confectioners' sugar.

Nest of Tropical Sorbets

Serves 4 to 6

This is one of my favorite desserts, a trio of mango, guava, and liliko'i sorbets in an almond tuile. Island flavors, low in fat, light, refreshing, goes well with any dish. Simple. Perfect.

ALMOND TUILE NEST

1/2 cup unsalted butter

3/4 cup sugar

1/2 cup corn syrup

1 1/4 cups cake flour

1 cup sliced almonds

MANGO SORBET

2 cups mango puree

1 tablespoon freshly squeezed lemon juice

1 cup Sorbet Syrup (page 225)

1 cup water

GUAVA SORBET

2 cups guava puree

1 tablespoon freshly squeezed lemon juice

1 cup Sorbet Syrup (page 225)

1 cup water

LILIKO'I SORBET

2 cups liliko'i or passion fruit puree

1 tablespoon freshly squeezed lemon juice

1 cup Sorbet Syrup (page 225)

1 cup water

1 cup whipped cream, for garnish

Mint sprigs, for garnish

To make the tuiles, in the bowl of an electric mixer on medium speed, cream the butter and sugar until slightly fluffy, 4 to 6 minutes. Add the corn syrup and flour and mix until combined. Stir in the almonds by hand. Transfer the mixture onto a clean, dry surface and roll it into a 3-inch-diameter log. Wrap the log in parchment paper and freeze for 1 hour.

Preheat the oven to 350°. Line a baking sheet with parchment paper. Remove the log from the freezer and slice into 1¼-inch-thick rounds. Transfer the rounds to the prepared pan, about 6 inches apart, and bake for 12 to 15 minutes, or until golden brown. While still

(continued)

continued from page 232

warm and malleable, and using a thin-bladed, wide metal spatula, drape the tuiles, one at a time, over a rolling pin to shape. When completely cool, store in an airtight container. If the tuiles harden too quickly, return to the 350° oven for 2 to 3 minutes, until malleable enough to shape.

To make the mango sorbet, in a bowl, combine all the ingredients. Transfer to an ice cream machine and process and freeze according to manufacturer's instructions.

To make the guava sorbet, in a bowl, combine all of the ingredients. Transfer to an ice cream machine and process and freeze according to manufacturer's instructions.

To make the liliko'i sorbet, in a bowl, combine all of the ingredients. Transfer to an ice cream machine and process and freeze according to manufacturer's instructions.

To serve, spoon whipped cream in the center of each plate. Top with a tuile nest. Place 1 scoop of each sorbet into each nest. Garnish each with 1 mint sprig.

Melon Ice with Tapioca and Banana

Serves 4 to 6

Tapioca is often served with fresh melon. The ice is a creative way of combining those ingredients that work so well together. Our Island bananas are so good, they add yet another flavor dimension to this dessert. It works particularly well with Asian food.

MELON ICE

4 cups diced ripe cantaloupe or
    honeydew melon

2 cups sugar

Juice of 2 limes

TAPIOCA

$1/2$ cup medium-pearl tapioca

$1\,1/2$ cups cold water

$4\,1/2$ cups half-and-half

3/4 cup sugar

3 eggs

1 teaspoon vanilla extract

4 medium bananas, sliced

Mint sprigs, for garnish

To make the ice, combine the melon, sugar, and lime juice in a blender and puree until smooth. Strain the mixture through a fine-mesh sieve. Transfer to an ice cream machine and process and freeze according to manufacturer's instructions.

To make the tapioca, in a bowl, soak the tapioca in the cold water for 2 hours. Strain the tapioca into another bowl and add the half-and-half. In a saucepan large enough to hold the bowl with the tapioca mixture, bring water to a simmer over medium heat. Place the bowl over the pot of water. In a separate bowl, combine the sugar, eggs, and vanilla and whisk lightly. Add the sugar mixture to the tapioca and cook until thickened, 20 to 25 minutes. Cover and set aside to cool.

Fold the banana into the tapioca. To serve, spoon the tapioca into martini or coupe glasses and top with 1 scoop of melon ice and 1 mint sprig.

Lychee Champagne Granité

Serves 4 to 6

Lychee is one of those wonderful Island fruits that's so plentiful in bumper crop years, you may find them in bags and boxes along the road just begging to be taken. It's always good to have a lychee tree in your yard . . . or at least in your neighbor's yard! The flavor is distinctive and super refreshing. This dessert can easily be used as an intermezzo, too.

40 fresh lychee, skinned and pitted

1 cup champagne or sparkling wine

1/2 cup sugar

Juice of 2 lemons

Mint sprigs, for garnish

Set aside 4 to 6 lychees. In a blender, combine the remaining lychees, 2 cups water, the champagne, sugar, and lemon juice and puree for 30 to 40 seconds. Pour the mixture into a 10-inch square pan and freeze overnight. Using the edge of a large spoon, scrape the frozen mixture to create a fluffy ice. Scoop the mixture into chilled martini glasses and garnish each one with 1 reserved lychee and 1 mint sprig.

Index